*For my family, near and far,
and to George and Big D who are probably
off eating Kincaid's burgers somewhere.*

*"There may be a lot of new research in veterinary medicine but there's still no cure for terminal dumbass!"*

-George W. Platt, DVM

*I enjoyed reading Horse Vet, Chronicles of a Mobile Veterinarian by Dr. Courtney Diehl. It is an easy read with real life stories of what to expect as a horse vet. I think anyone considering the idea of becoming a veterinarian should read this book. It will paint a picture of the realities, joys, and challenges that come with being a mobile horse veterinarian. These are experiences that are unique and, as she describes, "you just can't make up." I enjoyed this book and would recommend it.*

-Jacob Butler CJF, AWCF
of Butler Professional Farrier School LLC

*Not being a vet, a farrier, a trainer, barn manager or horse owner, I would've missed this book...and I'd have been sorry, because it's a GREAT read! I only stopped reading to fix lunch."*

-Cynthia Clark, Member of Bluebonnet
Equine Humane Society, former instructor with
Handicapped Equine Learning Program
and indulgent owner of some rescued dogs

# Table of Contents

Dr. Diehl and Cirrus, a BLM Mustang

# Introduction

I set out to write this book for a number of reasons. Being a vet was always my dream, and in many ways I feel fulfilled by what I do and cannot imagine a different career. Like many professions, there is a colorful mixture of good, bad or plain ugly experiences. People, personalities and other outside influences affect the trajectory of one's day, creating situations that range from incredibly funny to completely humiliating, and out of these come stories that you just can't make up. After hearing people tell me for years that I needed to write a book, I finally sat down and did it.

When I was a newer veterinarian, I did not realize how powerless I would be over certain situations with clients. A negative interaction with someone not only had the power to wreck my day, but sometimes my entire week. We routinely deal with medical situations that do not behave as expected, and the client's expectations are often not in line with reality despite our efforts to educate them. Sometimes clients become irrational and toxic and a situation that seemed under control quickly goes out of control. Conversely, some clients surprise me with reserves of wisdom, trust and support. The pendulum swings both ways, and I tell stories representative of both types of situations in this book.

I will also discuss spiritual faith and prayer, recognizing that this can be a touchy subject for some. Aggressive approaches to matters of spirituality and faith are off-putting, and so is disrespect to the religions of others. I will not shy away from discussing my relationship with God and prayer, in the hope that it may be helpful to others who have struggled with similar things, and I hope readers find my approach to be a welcoming one. I was not raised in a religious family, and I came to find faith on my own when I was still an undergraduate. I will say this: Had I not embraced faith in a higher power and sought help with situations that I could not manage on my own, I believe I would have come very close to a mental breakdown of some sort.

One aspect of veterinary medicine that is not discussed very often is the high suicide rate among veterinarians. How could this be, you ask? Veterinarians are kind, compassionate people who dedicate their lives to helping animals. What could be a more rewarding career choice? Everyone wants to be a veterinarian. People confide to me weekly their unrealized dreams of becoming an animal doctor.

Many people have said to me, "You must just LOVE animals!" Well, of course I do. But I didn't become a veterinarian because I love animals any more than a person becomes a pediatrician because they love children. I became a veterinarian because I love medicine and science, and I derive great joy from using my training to help creatures who cannot tell us where it hurts.

These voiceless creatures, however, come with humans attached to them. The veterinarian who explains that he went into animal medicine because he just doesn't like people had better think twice. Your life is now about the people who own your patients, and their understandings and expectations of the outcome of your medicine and surgery.

While most clients are mentally sound, you will find a solid percentage with various personality disorders that you now must cope with as you enter their lives and treat the creature they hold most dear, be it horse, rat, cat or snake.

You have now also entered a world of superstition, internet education, trainers and breeders who dole out medical advice, rampant mythology, and base prejudice that can warp even the sanest of clients and cause them to lose their trust in their veterinarian.

Is it any wonder that some veterinarians, defined and judged by often uneducated and unstable horse and pet owners, fall into career despair? Add in the impossible debts, ridiculous hours, lengthy drives, long phone calls, hard, sweaty labor, neglected families and pets, and lack of a personal life, and you have a veterinarian who just might be ready to cut off his own ear. Or take his own life. I hope that perhaps some of my colleagues will read this book and know that they are not alone. Perhaps sharing my faith and how I coped with specific toxic situations will be helpful to some. Perhaps it will even save someone's life!

I was blessed to have an excellent mentor early in my career, something I highly recommend to all new veterinarians. I also did an internship and a fellowship, something I don't necessarily recommend as highly – I am glad that I went through the experiences, as I learned many new things, but financially, it made no difference to my career, except to set me back even further. Having a mentor, a senior veterinarian who cares about you personally as well as professionally, makes all the difference. We cannot do this on our own, and we should not have to!

Like many veterinarians, I am often asked by eager twenty-somethings for veterinary career advice. Their earnest expressions and solemn declarations of love for animals are consistent, and there is usually a mom in there somewhere informing me that "Brittany has wanted to be a vet since she was little!" as Brittany nods enthusiastically and the two look expectantly at me, as though I alone hold the key to getting Brittany into vet school.

I can relate completely. I was the clichéd kid who read James Herriot and had a moment of total clarity about her career choice while sitting on her purple bedspread in a bedroom decorated with Duran Duran posters and puffy rainbow mobiles. I was going to be a vet and that was that, and I treated most vets that I met with hero worship.

When a kid has a dream that solid it is going to be extremely difficult to derail, and this book is not intended to derail anyone's dreams. I believe that having a dream and following it is one of the most essential things about growing up and figuring out how to make sense of this life we've been given. But dreams need to be tempered with facts. I hope that I can provide a balanced look inside the life of a mobile equine veterinarian in the 21st century and bring a dose of reality to those who wish to enter the veterinary profession.

# Nasticles

The man seemed nice enough on the phone, and it was refreshing to hear a male voice for a change, as so many of my horse clients were women. The conversation centered around the man's cutting horses and his breeding operation, and he was excited that some of the horses he'd sold were starting to perform well in the national events.

He wanted to discuss one horse in particular, a gelding named Smart Peppy Dualgun. This gelding was one of the most valuable and talented horses he'd ever seen and he'd seen quite a few. He also knew how knowledgeable I was about great horses, and how I had a good eye and was an excellent judge of quality. In fact, he'd heard that I was a superior cutting horse vet and a great person too.

It was lovely to have my many talents recognized, and I glowed under the praise. But it finally occurred to me to wonder why the horse had been castrated if he was as superior as described. And when, exactly, had I become a world-class cutting horse veterinarian?

As though on cue, the man asked his next question.

"What are those implant things called? Nasticles?"

I paused. "Nasticles? Oh, Neuticles! You mean the artificial testicle?"

"Yep, those. Can you put 'em in my horse? We want to show him as a stallion."

My jaw dropped. Perhaps this would be a good time to mention the fact that altering horses for show was completely unethical and illegal. Plus impregnating mares obviously would be impossible and this was usually the goal of showing a horse as a stallion. Was he also planning to sell semen from another stud under a false identity?

In the past, I'd been asked to block tails, inject joints with Silicon, provide off-label drugs, and alter paperwork. As I valued my vet license as well as my personal integrity, my answer was always in the negative. But this was a new one and I was a little speechless.

"I don't think they come in horse sizes," I finally said, stupidly.

"Well how big can you get them?"

"Uhh ..."

"Or we could just use rubber balls or something."

"Well, you see ..."

"Honey, the show world deserves this horse! Everyone who told me about you said you'd be the first to understand that! Little ladies are usually pretty reasonable, I've learned! Now when can you do him?"

That loosened my tongue.

"Sir, I will not be implanting artificial testicles into your horse so that you can show him as a stallion! I do not perform unethical veterinary services, and I don't know who would have told you that I did!" I was breathing fast and my face was beet red. "And you do not call me Honey! I can't help you and I recommend that you think very carefully before you get yourself banned from future competitions!"

My hand shook as I clenched the phone. The other end of the line was quiet for a moment. Then he chuckled.

"OK, OK, now don't get all worked up, sweetheart. I understand. You don't know how to do the surgery. You could have just told me that in the first place. So how about you recommend me someone who can. Just call me back with their number!"

I hung the phone up, teeth gritted. In five minutes I had gone from brilliant vet and excellent judge of horses to co-conspirator in crime, Little Lady, incompetent vet, and finally, receptionist.

Although I knew this man would probably never call me again, his name went onto the "list" in my vet software, and ominous warnings would pop up if his name were entered anywhere.

It seemed redundant, for I knew I wouldn't forget him anytime soon.

# Welcome to Private Practice!

This is what it's like to be a horse vet. You worked really hard to get into vet school. You labored for four years as a vet student, generated large student loan debt, and probably did an internship at an equine hospital for a year after graduation, where you made little to no money and worked ridiculous hours in hope that the hard labor would lead to a high-paying job.

In reality, your first job post-internship might have paid $40,000 annually, with promises of higher earnings as you "built up your position to full time." You probably worked on commission, which meant that the senior vets in your practice got all the high-paying calls, and you drove long distances to vaccinate and draw blood on horses. Maybe you were told that you'd receive a special bonus at the end of the year for overtime hours worked. More than likely that check never appeared.

You might not have realized until after you signed the long associate contract, over half of which was a severely restrictive non-compete clause covering most of the state in which the clinic was located, that the vet turnover in this practice was high, and that you were the fourth associate in less than two years to fill this position. Maybe you didn't notice that the practice owner was in his fifties and tended to sleep with staff members when his wife wasn't looking, while all of the associates were recent graduates and overwhelmingly female. You were probably referred to as the young vet, the new vet, the intern by the clients. Most of them called you by your first name right away, yet always addressed the senior vets as Doctor.

If you were the right person, you might eventually have gotten accepted by the senior vets and the clients. You moved up in the practice and began to earn a little more. If you were lucky, you had a spouse who stuck with you through vet school and could help you financially so that you could send a large amount of your paycheck to your student loan carrier every month and not worry about how you were going to pay the rest of the monthly bills. The long hours at work and on call were OK with your spouse, or maybe you weren't married, so it didn't matter. Your dog was a little neglected, but aside from not having any sort of a life outside of work, it was OK. You were happy your career was moving forward.

If you were unlucky, you showed up to work, accepted the low-paying calls that the front desk sent your way, wrote up your records, worked late thinking it would pay off in recognition and acceptance, then realized that it was one year later, you weren't making much more than when you started, and you seemed to be on call all the time. The "overtime bonus check" never materialized, nor did the practice owner have any recollection of discussing that with you. Doing fun things outside of work seemed like a distant memory. Plus, you just didn't feel that you fit in with the practice and the odds of becoming a partner seemed nonexistent. There was a huge age difference between you and the senior vets, and you felt that they just weren't current on a lot of the new technologies, nor were they interested in learning about them.

If you protested the on-call schedule, you were told that you had expressed a desire to earn more money, and this was a good way to do it. Meanwhile, your spouse, frustrated by your long hours and lower than anticipated pay, has started making noises about how unappreciated you are in this practice, and maybe it's time to look for another job in a better place.

The problem is that there is no better place and no better job. Moving to the dream job in the dream town is a rainbow that you'll chase, never to capture. Maybe you've already tested this theory and have a dossier of one or two failed jobs that you've neglected to list on your resume, instead finding creative ways to fill in the missing dates.

You've probably watched the AAEP and AVMA job listserv for so long you could recite a list of the practices that pop up with alarming regularity. Their ads usually read, "Seeking associate for busy equine practice. New grads welcome. Salary dependent on experience." This translates to, "We will run you ragged and pay you next to nothing." Or they might read, "Growing practice seeks motivated associate to build equine portion." This translates to, "We've realized that we can pay you next to nothing and capture a corner of the equine market that we know little about. Oh, and we still develop X-rays in a defunct bathroom."

When you're a horse vet working for a group practice, your reality is long hours, hard work, good colleagues and bad ones, some great clients, some toxic clients, and low pay. Either accept it and try to be happy, while working another job to pay your mounting bills, or move on to a different profession.

So you decide to stay put in your current situation and make the best of it. You labor to prove yourself to the horse people on whom you depend to make a living, the often emotionally unstable horse enthusiasts who become judge, jury, and executioner to your professional reputation, and consequently to your self-esteem. You seek professional validation from those not qualified to give it, and you turn yourself inside out to do a great job on their horses and get them to like and trust you. Sometimes you succeed.

You stay current on the latest new research and techniques in equine medicine. You fly off to conferences, spending money you don't have on plane tickets, hotel rooms and rental cars. You practice medical procedures until you can do them flawlessly, for there is no "backstage" in the horse vet world.

Often the first time you perform a certain procedure on a horse, a pastern injection, a tracheotomy in the field, you'll have an audience of horse owners, trainers, farriers and barn staff watching your every move, and some of them have worked with well-seasoned vets for years. Of course you do not tell them that you've never done this before on a live horse, only on a cadaver. You could win an Oscar for the performance you're about to deliver.

You learn to fake a phone call so you can run to the truck and look up something in the coffee-stained textbooks that bounce around on the front seat. You stay up late into the night with your patients, suture terrible lacerations in the cold, hike to horses with broken legs and lacerated tendons, drive your vet truck on rugged jeep tracks, breaking bottles of expensive drugs on the way. You leave your family early in the morning to attend a bad foaling, only to lose the mare and the foal. You return home after dark to a hungry family, unfolded laundry and a messy house.

And don't forget your debts. Remember those student loans that you blithely signed and signed for throughout vet school? Remember how you took every penny offered, thinking that you'd live frugally and not use it all, or maybe use it to make a payment toward the ever-mounting interest on your loans? Remember the loan consolidation paperwork at the end of your junior year? Everyone else was filling it out, so you did too, never thinking to research other consolidation options.

Well, repayment has kicked in! If you are even close to typical, you'll be coughing up anywhere from $1,500 to $2,500 a month. And since you locked in your interest rates when you consolidated, welcome to the sad fact that most of what you carve from your slim monthly salary goes directly to loan interest, not principal, guaranteeing that student loan repayments are probably going to be forever.

One day you look up and you've been at it for thirteen years. Your debt hasn't budged and your body is tired, and you're approaching burnout. You don't have any other job skills and you've been away from small animal medicine for so long that it would be malpractice if you went back now. Yet you love a lot of what you do and can't imagine doing anything else!

# Which leg is it?

As the horse moves off, I'm baffled for a minute. Left front? Right hind? No, it's his neck! Oh crap, he's neurologic!

Then I remember. He's a Tennessee Walking horse, and since they move like eggbeaters, I need to condition my eye to his gaits before I can pick out the leg responsible for the lameness.

The owner runs ahead of him down the driveway, a paddock full of enthusiastic eggbeaters following along on the other side of the fence. Bemusedly, the horse ambles along behind the man, forelimbs in one gait, hind limbs in another. His head and neck are extended in response to the strong pull of the lead rope, and the owner looks as though he's running into a stiff wind in slow motion. They travel exactly 10 yards and he stops and looks at me expectantly.

"Well? Which leg is it? " he puffs.

"He needs to go a little farther," I explain. "I can't really tell."

I endure a lecture about how Tennessee Walkers are gaited horses and they do not move like regular horses, and I need to understand that. He tries again to jog the horse, briefly tangling his feet in the lead rope and colliding with the horse's shoulder. The animal skitters sideways, speeds up, slows down, travels diagonally, then skids to a stop. They cover 15 yards this time.

When I still can't pinpoint the lameness, the owner exhales in disgust.

"It's a pretty obvious lameness, Doc! I picked it out first thing this morning. Saw it from across the field! But I know these horses inside and out, and I know each one by how he moves. The Tennessee Walker is a gaited ..."

I interrupt and suggest we longe the horse, and immediately regret it, as I am subjected to another lecture about how Tennessee Walkers don't like longe lines. Or round pens. Or me. And if I were a Tennessee Walker person, I would know that.

I decide to punt and examine all four legs. Nothing. I examine all four feet. Nothing. I squeeze the soles of the feet with hoof testers, flex all joints, palpate all structures. Nothing. I'm stumped.

The man is looking over my shoulder, a strange look on his face, and I am braced for another verbal lashing about my ignorance of Tennessee Walkers and all things eggbeater. He opens his mouth, closes it, then taps his chin. Then he takes a deep breath.

"Doc, I think I brought you the wrong horse. This one just needs his teeth floated. "

# Mentorship

Courtney Diehl, DVM and George Platt, DVM looking at x-rays, 2003

Like many others, I fell into the "internship" trap. "Internship" in equine medicine often means a week or two of mentoring, then you're off on a long day of calls by yourself, and can also expect to handle most nights on call, as well as weekends, and also do all treatments and exams on any horses in the hospital. You'll get some perfunctory attention at times, when the other vets remember that you are accepting your 21k annual paycheck to actually receive some hands-on training, but it won't be consistent.

I was lucky to have a great mentor after my internship was over, an equine veterinarian by the name of George W. Platt, DVM. I met George when I visited some old friends in Vail, ironically, on a break from my internship. I was disillusioned by the veterinary world, having just left the practice's Christmas party, where the senior veterinarian in the practice handed out sex toys to the male vets as party favors. The female vets, mercifully, were ignored, and we leaned uncomfortably against the wall of the treatment room, waiting for a polite time to leave.

I was so happy to be back in Colorado and be away from the clinic for a while. It was like coming home, as I'd lived in the Vail area for years before attending vet school and had worked for Vail Associates as a lift operator, summer trail crew worker and, finally, running a snowcat. It was through the cat crew that I met George, as he was good friends with my old foreman, Britt.

One night I was visiting the shop, fondly known as the "catbox," and checking out the brand new Bombardier cats that Vail had just bought. Britt pressed George's number into my hand and insisted that I call him. I did immediately, and made plans to meet him the following day. George and I went out on a day of vet calls, Platt style, and got along really well. George asked me to join him after the internship was completed. He wasn't going to hire me per se, but would mentor me and support me as a new veterinarian and help me build up a practice.

My first day with George went something like this. I arrived early at his place in Edwards, Colorado, and rapped smartly on the door, dressed in pressed khakis, a button down shirt with "Dr. Courtney Diehl" embroidered on it, and a tidy satchel with my resume, cover letter, lunch and a drug formulary.

No answer. I knocked again, thinking I could hear bluegrass music.

After waiting a polite interval, I banged hard on the door, and it was finally yanked open by a lean, grinning man in his late sixties, with a stars and stripes baseball cap perched on his grey head. Bright blue eyes twinkled at me, and a warm, callused hand firmly grasped mine. I was tugged inside and studied head to toe.

"Hope you're ready to get dirty!" said George. He spoke with a Texas drawl. I noticed that he hadn't bothered with clean, pressed khakis, choosing instead a pair of Levis and an NRA T-shirt. His wife Cornelia greeted me warmly, a similar sparkle in her eyes. I had a cup of coffee and enjoyed a conversation with Cornelia as George bustled about getting ready and talking on the phone.

He finally piled his daybook on top of a battered metal clipboard, phone clamped in his mouth, and we climbed into a battered blue-green Ford vet truck with a rifle rack in the back window and Band-Aids all over the floor.

I sat on a pile of papers, two rectal sleeves, a roll of vet wrap and a pack of gum.

He waved his arm. "You can just shove all that on the floor!"

I obeyed, and the clutter joined a pair of pliers, pocket knife, towels, horse magazines and CD cases. I wasn't sure where to put my feet, so I parked them on either side of the pile. The roar of the diesel was fairly loud, but I figured we could talk over it.

"What are we seeing today, Dr. Platt?" I asked smartly, ready to be quizzed on my veterinary knowledge.

"Huh?" said George.

I took a deep breath and repeated my question loudly.

"Oh. It's supposed to snow, I think. Hope you brought warm

clothes." And he pushed a CD into the player and Dolly Parton assaulted my ears. I gave up trying to talk and flipped through a horse magazine.

Soon we were at our first call, and good intern that I was, I hopped out of the truck quickly, prepared to load the tote with the needed equipment. I couldn't find the tote, and I realized I still didn't know what we were doing. Carefully addressing him as Doctor, I asked again what we were doing.

He smiled. "Call me George. We're changing a bandage."

The patient was a fat roan mare with a taped up leg. George swiftly removed the bandage, expertly dodging her attempts to kick him, and just as quickly applied a new one. I tried to help, reaching down for a new roll of tape to hand him, but he was too quick. I got in the way more than I helped.

He was kind. "Next one will be more interesting. We're going to see a laminitis case that I've been treating for about 10 weeks. Had to resect this one but she's already back under saddle."

I stared. "I'm sorry. Resect?" I had no idea what he was talking about.

"Have you seen many laminitis cases, Courtney?"

Laminitis is a nasty disease of the horse's foot. It causes swelling and damage to the structure that anchors the foot bone inside the hoof capsule. Severe cases can result in separation of the bone and hoof wall, or the bone coming through the sole of the foot. We'd covered laminitis extensively in school and I'd done well on exams on the subject.

I straightened up, brimming with the current medical regimens, and went on to brag about the one case I'd seen and treated on my own, and how the horse had made a full recovery with all of the drugs I'd given it.

George studied me, then put a kind arm around my shoulders.

"That horse got well in spite of you, not because of you!"

I opened my mouth to argue, but he was already in the truck, Dolly Parton continuing where she'd left off. Bemused, I climbed in and we took off down the road, George not wearing his seatbelt. I tried a few more questions, and he tried to hear me, but after a while I gave up.

His phone rang a lot during the drive, and I listened with interest as he talked. He did turn the music down slightly.

"That's ridiculous! I never told her to do that! Of course that horse is sore now! Dang, one more neuron and she'd have a synapse! Tell her to cut that out!"

"Well, I don't have a page in my book for 'the next time I'm out that way.' I'll put you down for Tuesday." And he'd write in his careful script, "Float Teeth, Vera Petersen" on the page for Tuesday, never taking his eyes off the road, phone tucked to his ear.

Then he sat up straighter. "How bad? No, I don't want you to walk him up and down the road. If he wants to lie down, let him lie down! I'm headed your way!"

He hung up the phone and looked at me. "We've got a colic. The next call can wait." And he quickly dialed his phone, explained the situation to the next call, and we did a U-turn across two lanes of traffic and headed back the way we'd come. Colic was the horseman's term for belly ache and it could mean anything from a gas cramp to a potentially fatal intestinal problem.

"Don't walk those colics around. If your belly hurts, what do you want to do? You want to lie down! And so do they! Let them lie down! And those owners always want to give Banamine! Don't let them give the horse anything. All that'll do is mask the problem and then you and I can't do our job! We'll give the Banamine if necessary!"

It took me a minute to realize that he was talking to me, not the telephone. I decided this was not the time to tell him how many hours I had spent in vet school and on my internship walking colics around, so I nodded sternly and tried to look as though I'd never ever walk a colic around or let an owner give Banamine. Banamine is a non-steroidal-anti-inflammatory drug commonly used to treat pain, and it is popular in colic treatment.

"Can't they develop an intestinal torsion if they are allowed to roll?" I asked timidly. This was what I had been taught. A torsion is a twist somewhere in the intestines, requiring surgery to correct.

"Oh bullshit! People need to stop believing that nonsense. They can twist in cross ties or tied up in a trailer. What's the point of exhausting them dragging them up and down the driveway? They're tired, they hurt, and they want to lie down!"

Soon we were pulling into the driveway where the colicky horse waited. George exploded into action. I tried to help but couldn't find anything on his truck, and in quick succession he had sedated the horse, performed a rectal exam, passed a stomach tube and was pumping something into the tube.

I held the bucket.

"Dr. Platt, what are you giving the horse?" asked the owner.

"Mag sulfate and water," said George, who looked at me wickedly, then proceeded to tell one of the most off-color jokes about bowel function I have ever heard.

The owner howled. I wanted to laugh too, but I was desperate to seem professional. I kept a solemn face as I asked George if he would also give mineral oil, as it was commonly used on colicky horses. He kept pumping as he spoke.

"How long does it take for oil to break down an impaction? Tell you what. Put a dry manure ball into a bucket of oil, and call me when it's dissolved. I'll put one in a bucket of water and mag sulfate and I'll call you when it's dissolved." He turned to the owner. "Who's getting called first?"

The owner smiled at me.

George continued. "But I like oil. It lubricates my stomach pump!" And he poured a dollop into his bucket.

The horse was much more comfortable and as we packed up the truck, George quizzed me on certain colic problems and how I would treat them. I was too shy to ask what mag sulfate was, so I looked it up when I got home. It was Epsom salts.

Next stop was the laminitis case and I got my first look at a heart bar shoe and a resected foot. In this particular horse, the foot bone, or pedal bone, had torn away from the hoof wall inside of the foot, resulting in a wedge of stretched, dead lamina between the structures. On the X-rays, you could see how much rotation had occurred.

Removal of the hoof wall and all of the dead tissue meant that the pedal bone, supported by the heart bar shoe, could move back into a normal position and the new hoof wall could grow down against the pedal bone. George wasn't "band-aiding" laminitis. He was fixing it.

The horse trotted in from the field and bounced around at the gate while the owner put on the halter. The feet looked as though windows had been carved into the toes, and I didn't see any wraps or bandages anywhere.

George knocked on the resected toe with the butt of his hoof pick. "See how it's all hardened up? This horse is barrel racing with these resected feet."

The owner beamed. "I was pretty freaked out when Dr. Platt cut her hoof walls away, but she'd been lame for months and he fixed her! I have my horse back thanks to him! We won first place in last week's rodeo!"

George lifted the foot to show me the heart bar shoe. It was a shoe with a closed heel and a frog plate, and it did look a little like a heart. The frog is the triangular-shaped structure in the center of the horse's sole. He explained that using the frog of the foot to help support the horse's weight was the basic premise for how the shoe worked and why it eased the pain of the laminar disease.

By supporting the frog, the pedal bone was also supported and the strain was minimized on the lamina. But the frog support had to be perfect. Too much and it would make the horse worse. Too little and the shoe wouldn't help. A poorly fitted frog plate could put sole pressure on the foot, which would be painful to the horse. A skilled horseshoer, known as a farrier, was a critical part of the equation for treating laminitis George's way.

"Make friends with the farriers, Courtney. If you want a successful practice, that's the smartest thing you can do! You can't do your job without a good vet-farrier partnership!"

I asked about pain medications and immediately regretted it, as his enthusiastic lecture quickly turned into outraged bellowing, the amused owner taking it all in. Clearly she'd had this directed at her too, and was glad to see someone else in the hot seat.

"Why would you give a foundered horse Bute?" George fumed. Phenylbutazone, known as Bute, is a popular pain medication used in horse care.

"You don't want him standing when his feet hurt! You want him to lie down! If he lies down, the damage to the feet stops! The horse knows what he needs to do and people are too damn stupid to let him do it! If you want to see a laminitis become a sinker, give the horse Bute! He'll keep standing and then those bones will come right out the bottom of the foot. I've never seen a sinker that wasn't on Bute!"

Sinker syndrome is the most feared complication that a laminitic horse can develop. "Sinkers" occur when the attachments to the foot bone fail completely and the bone descends through the sole of the foot. Sinkers have a very low survival rate.

George spoke from experience. George and a well-known farrier named Burney Chapman, CJF, had resurrected the heart bar shoe from an 1800s shoeing manual and had enjoyed tremendous success in treating laminitic horses. George had worked for a number of insurance adjusters and had flown all over the country to use his methods. In the mid-1980s, he and Burney presented their findings at the American Association of Equine Practitioners (AAEP) annual vet conference. George had been the subject of multiple magazine articles and was also in the International Equine Practitioner's Hall of Fame.

It was interesting that I had never been exposed to these methods in vet school, but suddenly I realized that I knew exactly who Dr. Platt was! Some of the vets from back east had referenced him on a famous horse that he and Burney had treated. The horse had returned to successful competition, and the story was still being told far and wide. I realized that I had even read the paper they'd written and it all clicked together in my mind.

I suddenly felt very young and very foolish.

Nearly every laminitis case I'd ever seen had been on multiple pain medications. Some had an IV line in and were hooked up to a pump to deliver the drugs constantly. Icing the feet had become fashionable, and we'd spent hours refilling the ice slurry in the rubber boots that were buckled around the horse's legs. The horses were either barefoot or they wore a special thick-soled boot called Soft Rides. Many became sinkers in the hospital.

No one put shoes on a laminitis case in the beginning. Some clinicians had very strong arguments about pounding on the feet and causing the horse more pain, and this was the rationale for avoiding shoes.

I'd also never seen a laminitis case lie down in the hospital, and what George was saying made tremendous sense. Standing and moving around on a weakened lamina could only cause more damage. Supporting the foot with a heart bar shoe and letting the horse lie down seemed completely logical to me. But it flew directly in the face of everything I'd been taught. I'd have to think about this.

George had called into question a number of things that I thought were established facts in veterinary science. I had been humbled multiple times throughout the day and it was clear that he knew what he was doing, yet there wasn't a trace of superiority or glee in putting me in my place. This man truly cared about horses, and he possessed not only knowledge but wisdom. This was someone I wanted to learn from, and suddenly I badly wanted to come to Colorado and work with him.

Before long it was done. I finished my internship and returned to Colorado. George helped me outfit my vet truck and slowly my phone started to ring. If I wasn't busy, which I often wasn't, I would tag along with George and learn as much as I could.

We spent many days palpating mares for pregnancy, something I wasn't great at. You lube up your arm and go in rectally, trying to locate the uterus and feel a swelling on one of the uterine horns. George had done a lot of repro in Texas, and to him it was no big deal, but I had been very frustrated by my poor palpation skills and was anxious to improve.

George had a theory about that.

"It's those thick palpation sleeves you use! If you want to learn to check a mare, you've got to do it barehanded."

He arranged to have me join him on a half day of preg-checking mares at a barn where we both worked, and greeted me with a bucket of warm water and a bar of Ivory soap. There were no rectal sleeves in sight. I had recently begun dating a photographer from Texas named Jim, and he came along with us, camera in hand.

I looked doubtfully at the soap, then down at my clean white T-shirt. Usually I clipped the rectal sleeve to my shoulder to keep out the manure. George was pulling on a nylon garment that had obviously seen a lot of use, and it covered his shirt completely. He enthusiastically soaped his arm. I did the same, minus the enthusiasm. George would check the mare first, barehanded, then let me palpate her and we'd compare findings. Jim proceeded to take some of the most disgusting pictures of me that I have ever seen! We married four years later – I figured he had to be the right guy if he still wanted to be with me after that experience!

I tried not to make a face as I slid my bare arm into the mare's rectum, but quickly forgot my distaste when the pregnant uterus slid against my fingertips. Suddenly it was easy and I was able to find all of the pregnancies fairly quickly. I couldn't believe it!

I thought of all of the fumbling around I'd done over the last year, finding nothing but manure balls, then offering a wild guess to the clinician I was working with. I'd also spent hours trying to learn to ultrasound the mares rectally. We used a slim probe as long as my finger, and I'd wave it around inside the mare until my arm was exhausted, occasionally finding the structure that eluded me. For the first time in my vet career, I was enjoying repro!

George admitted that he didn't use the ultrasound very much, but he was willing to give it a try. His palpation skills were so finely tuned that he could reliably detect an 18-day pregnancy, something I still can't do without the ultrasound. With this technology, we can now detect a 14-day pregnancy, and vets today are very dependent on the ultrasound for repro work. I always palpate first, then check my result with the ultrasound. It has improved my palpation skills tremendously, but George remains the master.

My arm was deep green when I got home that night and smelled evil for days, despite repeated scrubbing with lemon juice, bleach and toothpaste. But I didn't care. I could preg-check a mare!

# Mobile Life

Dr. Diehl at work in a typical Colorado winter 2012

I have been a mobile vet for most of my career. While I have spent my share of time in clinics and hospitals, I prefer being outside and I love driving around the country. My large truck easily accommodates all of my equipment, my husband, two car seats and two little girls. The powerful diesel engine gets me over the steep mountain passes and the truck is steady in most kinds of weather.

Most mobile vets drive either a Suburban or some type of truck to allow space for the variety of equipment we must carry. There are vehicle inserts for the travelling doctor, and they range from a chest of drawers that bolts into the back of the Suburban to a full fiberglass unit that fits into the pickup bed. These truck units are usually equipped with hot and cold water, electric lights and even a refrigerator.

Although there is a large vet symbol on the back of the white unit, it still confuses people. Like many horse vets, I have yet to put a professional sign on my vehicle. One of these days I will buy one and simplify my life. I have been mistaken for an ice cream truck, an electrician, and the Schwan's man. Once an old man pointed at the truck bed and asked me for four fresh trout.

Some, seeing the vet symbol, are interested and come over to chat and I have met many of my clients this way. Others, oblivious to the fact that I need to be somewhere else, see me as a form of entertainment. I am either a captive audience for every vet story they can remember, or the contestant on Stump the Chump.

Alpaca people are often the worst.

I was parked at a gas station, indulging in my usual late-lunch hotdog, when a heavyset woman approached the truck and thumped on the window. My newspaper was propped onto my steering wheel, and I had a mouthful of food. I had to fumble the keys into the ignition to roll the window down, and my newspaper slid into my lap in a jumble of papers.

It was hard not to feel a little resentful at having my lunch disturbed, and her tone of voice didn't help.

"Do you know anything about alpacas? Vets usually don't!" she barked at me accusingly.

Swallowing my food, I sat up a little straighter, prepared to amaze her with my alpaca knowledge.

"Why, yes, I do ..."

She interrupted, and started a long discourse on alpaca veterinary care. It wasn't much of a conversation, but I was able to insert an occasional sentence fragment.

She continued. "Ever heard of Hemingway?"

I swallowed some hotdog, caught off guard by being allowed to speak. "Yes, of course ..." Hemingway was a famous alpaca herdsire.

She looked at me triumphantly.

"How about Accoyo Rex's Majesty Majestic?"

I had to admit that I hadn't.

"He's a great, great grandson of Hemingway and I have a girl bred to him this year!"

An alpaca pedigree including a distant connection to Hemingway was like a Thoroughbred horse pedigree claiming Bold Ruler or Man O' War, but I decided against pointing this out.

The woman started another long story about how the last vet wasn't prepared to do an emergency C-section on a female who had been in labor for a day and a half. The dam, a daughter of Maxine's Booming Blooming Blossom, and cria, by General Admiral Luster Buster, both died and it was all the vet's fault.

I tried unsuccessfully to defend the luckless vet. Then I sealed my fate by admitting that I had heard of neither of these great alpacas.

Tempting as it was to launch into a long detailed defense of my profession, it was clear that if I continued to engage with this woman, I would be guaranteed nothing more than a starring role in her next tale about incompetent veterinarians. There was no benefit in continuing this verbal jousting and my short lunch break was over. I had to head to my next appointment.

She ignored my attempts to end the conversation. I tried looking at my watch, opening my daybook and pointing to my next call, and finally I started my diesel truck, hoping the noise would drown her out. But this lady was built to talk over a diesel and she kept right on.

Defeated, I put the truck in gear and started to ease it backwards. She kept pace with me, still talking, and in a flash of inspiration I interrupted her long enough to hand over the number of a colleague who constantly stuck me with all of her emergency calls. I made sure to tell the woman what an alpaca expert this vet was.

She was already dialing her cell phone as I drove away. Yes, these chance meetings with people were useful indeed.

# The Farm Call Discussion

*Client: Well, you charge a farm call. What do I get for the farm call?*

*Me: The farm call covers my travel mileage, vehicle and vet unit expenses and time.*

*Client: How many exams do I get for that?*

*Me: The farm call doesn't cover the exams or any other work I do.*

*Client: The farm call just gets you there?*

*Me: The farm call just gets me there.*

*Client: Well, what if I came and got you?*

*Me: Well, I need the vet truck you see...*

*Client: Because it doesn't cost me that to just come and get you!*

*Me: I think you're missing the point ...*

*Client: I'm not made of money you know!*

*Me: I'm sorry but these are standard charges in the vet industry. And you can't come and get me. It doesn't work that way.*

*Client: Well, once you're at my place, all you'll be seeing are rescue horses. You discount those, right?*

*Me: No.*

*Client: But I rescued them and spent my own money to save their lives! I'm not made of money, you know!*

*Me: Yes, you did mention that earlier ...*

*Client: I think I'll just do their shots myself. That'll save me money.*

*Me: Excellent idea.*

*Client: Can I buy them from you? If I buy in bulk, I get a discount, right?*

# Regarding Horse Castrations

Horse castrations are a normal part of any horse vet's practice. Typically they are done on the farm, and can be performed with the horse standing or laying down under general anesthesia. The size and temperament of the patient usually dictates which method is used. For obvious reasons, I preferred my standing procedures to be performed on smaller, quieter horses.

They don't teach the standing procedure in vet schools very often. It was popular in the 1970s, but as general anesthetics improved, the procedure faded in popularity. There are safety concerns with it as well; I was once kicked in the knee by a large yearling being prepped for a standing castration. The yearling was quickly gelded by George, who, ironically, was teaching me the procedure that day. George could geld a horse in five minutes flat and had an admiring crowd around him. I went to the hospital with a fractured tibia.

Despite the risks, I do many of them standing, as there can also be a risk with general anesthesia. Clients often ask for standing, fearing complications with laying their horse down, and are surprised and pleased when I offer it as an option.

The caller on the phone was clear about her preferences.

"I don't want them laid down! They are gentle as can be, and you can do them standing!"

28

"Them" referred to two enormous 4-year-old Warmblood stallions. My head did not quite reach the top of the withers of the first horse, and when I went to palpate the testicles to be sure that both were descended, he pinned his ears, lashed his tail, and a hind leg whipped through the air, barely missing me. The second horse was even larger, and even more ill-mannered.

"I'm sorry, but I'm not going to be able to castrate these horses standing. For safety reasons, I will have to lay them down," I told the owner, listing all the reasons why standing would be too dangerous. Eventually she agreed, and on the appointed day, my assistant and I were ready for them. Jillian was a vet student and had a lot of experience in field anesthesia.

We had picked a flat area in a large field and all of the drugs and instruments were ready. The owner stood to the side, lead rope and halter draped over her shoulder, and did not seem to be in a hurry to produce our first patient.

"OK, we're ready!" I finally said.

She slowly turned and walked down a long hill toward a paddock with about eight huge Warmbloods chasing each other, rearing, air kicking, and just having a great time. With dismay, I recognized our two patients among the mob.

From our vantage point, we could see all the action, and our first patient showed little interest in being caught. He thundered up and down the fence line, twisting through the air like a comet, the owner lost among the plunging bodies. Occasionally we could see the top of her head, or a waving arm.

Jillian was rising to hike down and help, when the owner emerged from the herd with a haltered horse in hand. Still in the mood for trouble, he spun about her like a top, and when she opened the gate, he charged through it and skidded to a stop, lathered sides heaving. He screamed to his buddies the whole way up the hill, and when I gave him the first shot, meant to sedate him, it had little effect.

Adrenaline in the system causes most sedatives to work poorly or not at all, and I had given him almost double what I normally would have by the time his head dropped and his eyes half closed. We gave him plenty of time to "let the drugs soak in" before giving the second shot that would lay him down. His vitals were strong, heart rate at a low normal, and everything seemed fine.

Jillian injected the Ketamine and Valium combination into his vein and he went down perfectly, snoring deeply. We scrubbed and prepped the surgery site, and I injected a local anesthesia into and around the testicles. I made the cut into the scrotal skin and popped the first testicle out. Jillian craned her head around to see, and gasped at the size of it.

"Are you going to ligate the cord?" she asked.

I was. I didn't normally, but this cord was the diameter of my arm, and I didn't trust the emasculators to crush it properly. I wasn't used to ligating during a routine castration, as it wasn't always necessary, and it took me longer than it should have. Jillian stayed on top of the anesthesia, re-dosing him when he seemed to be getting light.

I had just finished tying off the second cord, when both of us saw his head move. In a flash, Jillian was on top of his neck, holding him flat, and frantically, I crushed and severed the ligated cord. The testicle came free, emasculators clamped firmly in place, and suddenly his legs were moving dangerously close to my face. I dove for his head as well, but he sat up, shaking us off effortlessly. Jillian and I collided, hauled his head back down, sat frantically on his neck, but he struggled to his feet, sprawling both of us in the dirt. My emasculators clanged between his legs as he weaved unsteadily.

My pants were ripped across one knee, I had a darkening swelling on my forearm, and Jillian's cheek was swollen. Our patient towered over us, trying to make sense of the world. We grabbed him and I shot another dose of sedative into his vein to keep him calm while he metabolized the general anesthetic still in his system. The owner danced around him making some kind of chirping noise that was supposed to soothe him.

He remained quiet as I removed the emasculators from the testicular cords, and no fresh bleeding was evident. We carefully moved him to a roomy stall for the recommended 24-hour clot time, and watched him for a while to make sure he would not bleed. All was well, and he was nibbling hay when we left.

Our surgery site was a disaster. Syringes and empty Ketamine and Valium bottles were everywhere, and my surgery pack had been flung across the field. I looked sadly at my crushed Powerfloat case that we had used as a surgery table.

Ten minutes of clean-up and scrubbing instruments in disinfectant solution, and we were ready for our second patient. I gave the owner a stern lecture about excitement before anesthesia, and she nodded silently as she went to go catch the horse.

It was a repeat of the first fiasco, only there was more dust and action, and mostly the owner disappeared from sight. Horse heads shot from the group, feet flew every which way, and the herd seemed to take on a single identity of menacing chaos. It seemed hours before our second patient appeared, dancing on his hind legs. The owner managed to get him through the gate, but he charged her, and she threw her hands into the air, dropping the lead rope to the ground.

Off went our patient at a furious gallop around a very large field. He disappeared over a ridge and was gone from sight for nearly a minute. The horse mob thundered around the paddock in approval, cheering him on. We spotted him at the bottom of the hill, a brown blur, lead rope flailing behind him, and as we watched, he completed one, two, then three complete laps around the field. Finally he pulled up outside the paddock where his companions waited, then began to run back and forth along the fence line trying to get back in.

The owner was able to catch him, and hauled him up the hill to us. He was soaked with sweat, every vein popping out under his skin, and he heaved frantic puffing breaths. I gave him fifteen minutes to calm down, and he seemed to, accepting the first sedative shot nicely.

Every vet has that moment of, "Hmmm, maybe I shouldn't do this right now." A wiser colleague seemed to be whispering in my ear to rethink what I was about to do, but I stupidly ignored my misgivings and proceeded.

Jillian looked at me questioningly but didn't say anything as I gave him the second shot to lay him down. As with the first shot, he was surprisingly cooperative, and I finished injecting the dose and stepped back, waiting for him to show signs of getting ready to go down.

He turned his head and stared at me as I watched him. A horse below him neighed and his ears flicked toward the sound. Then he bent his head and began cropping grass.

I waited longer. He seemed to stagger slightly, but caught himself quickly. I looked at my watch – four minutes since the shot had gone in. The owner began her chirping again, distracting him, and we had to ask her to stop.

Finally, his hindquarters wavered, and he dropped to the ground in a sitting position, front legs holding his chest off the ground. Jillian pushed him gently, and his forelimbs buckled, but his head stayed up. We were able to ease his head to the ground and cover his eye with a towel. Jillian re-dosed him immediately, and cautiously I began scrubbing his scrotum and blocking the testicles with local anesthetic. His hind leg would quiver and briefly lift in the air, and his tail would twitch as he felt the poke of the needle.

"I'm afraid to give him any more drugs!" Jillian hissed.

"How much has he had?" I whispered, and she named the dose – almost three times what a normal horse would take. We were still in the safety range for the drugs, but they just weren't having any effect on the horse.

We considered him, twitching, head under the towel. Cautiously I reached between his hind legs to check my local block, giving his testicles a firm tug. He didn't seem to react, but as I laid out my instruments, clanging stainless steel together, I saw his ear move, then his head lift, and suddenly he was standing, eating grass, towel still hanging from his halter.

"I have never seen that happen!" Jillian exclaimed. All I could do was stare at him in dismay.

We quickly checked the expiration dates for all of the drugs used. All were fine. The drugs had been stored properly, not getting too warm or too cold. Clearly trying to anesthetize him after all of the excitement had been a huge mistake and was certainly the reason for the failure of the drugs. I should have known better.

Still making chirping noises, the owner pulled the towel from the horse's halter, and he trotted briskly down the hill to his buddies, never missing a step.

Jillian and I sat together and watched him, humbled into silence.

Eventually she spoke. "Do Warmbloods process drugs differently than other horses?"

I laughed. "I think Warmbloods do everything differently. They can be very difficult to work on sometimes. But I shouldn't have tried to anesthetize him after all the excitement. This was my fault."

She nodded, and I cringed, envisioning her recounting this day to her anesthesiology professor. "And which vet did you say you were working with?" the professor would say. "Diehl? Diehl. Hmmm." And I would become a widely used example of what never to do in the field.

Jillian turned to me, her forehead creased, and I prepared for the debriefing of the disaster.

"Doc?" she said, anxiously. "How long will his testicles be numb?"

We returned the following day to check on the new gelding that was still in his stall. He was bright and eating, and there were only a few drops of blood in the shavings around his feet. Typically, new castrations are left in a confined space for 24 hours, and if all is well, are then moved to a larger area, and light exercise is started. I checked his vitals, and pronounced him ready to move to a larger space.

The owner haltered him and led him and us through a maze of gates and panels. I had carefully explained the management and aftercare necessary on the horse, and was sure that I had been clear. She opened a final gate and we all stepped through, Jillian fastening it firmly behind us. It seemed like a very large paddock, and somehow familiar, and as I opened my mouth to comment, she released the gelding and I was horrified to see the horse mob, including the numb patient from yesterday, thundering toward us. Our patient broke toward it into a rapid gallop and it enveloped him like a giant amoeba.

In a stunning replay of the day before, the mob spun, screamed, thundered terrifyingly close to us, broke apart and grouped together in great clouds of dust. Jillian and I flung our arms out to spare us from being trampled and screamed to the owner to catch the gelding before he started to bleed. He appeared right before us, sparring on his hind legs with one of his buddies. As I watched, a blood clot the size of an orange broke loose from his scrotum, and dark blood cascaded onto the ground, splattering his hind legs.

Somehow we were able to loop a rope around his neck, and we hurried him from the mob and right back to the same stall that we had taken him from. We left the owner somewhere in the stampede hoping she'd get trampled.

The hemorrhage had slowed to a steady fast drip as I sedated him, and I gloved up and cautiously explored my incisions from yesterday. I was able to locate both cords and was relieved to find the ligatures still tightly tied. To be safe, I clamped the cord ends with large hemostats and started him on antibiotics, in addition to the anti-inflammatories he was already getting.

He was calmly eating his hay when we left, but both of us were a mess, blood caking our boots, pant legs, my arm. My pulse rate took a very long time to return to normal.

Later in the week, the clinic that I sent the second stallion to for in-hospital gelding reported an easy, uneventful anesthesia induction with Ketamine and Valium, smooth castration and a nice normal recovery. They'd keep him for several days, and they'd do all of the controlled exercise and follow-up care. They said he was one of the better patients they'd had in a while.

# Congenital Problems

Another castration disaster came in the form of a half Welsh pony. The pony was gentle, and stood about 13 hands. I had checked his half-brother that day, and found that he only had one testicle. We call these horses "cryptorchids," meaning that one testicle remains somewhere in the abdomen, and it is a more involved surgical process to remove it. The owner made arrangements to take him into the clinic for castration. I wish she'd taken both in.

I checked out the remaining pony. He peered at me from underneath a turbulent explosion of forelock, and gentle brown eyes regarded me calmly. He did not protest as I palpated him. There were two testicles descended in the scrotum, and no other suspicious structures that could have indicated problems.

I had learned the hard way to do a testicle count before laying the horse down under general anesthesia, as it was mortifying to discover a cryptorchid after the horse was on the ground. All was well, and confidently I gave the combination of drugs to knock out the pony. He stood peacefully for the shot and I felt fortunate, as ponies are often very naughty with needles.

He went down perfectly, and after scrubbing the scrotum and injecting local anesthesia into the testicles, I gelded him quickly. I watched him carefully to make sure there was no excessive bleeding and checked his vitals, which were all fine.

The pony snored contentedly, showing no signs of waking, so the owner and I left him in his stall and went to vaccinate the rest of her horses.

We were probably gone for fifteen minutes, and when we returned, he was starting to move his ears and twitch his lips. I knew he'd be getting up soon, and the owner went in to check his incisions for any new bleeding. She stood over him, then frowned.

"Doc, he's protruding a little."

I assumed that she meant that the penis was dropping from the sheath, but went to check, as the look on her face worried me. I was horrified to see a handful of small intestine squirming free of the incisions over his scrotum. And he was starting to lift his head and strain a little, pushing more and more out!

I ran as fast as I could to the vet truck and seized more drugs to knock him back out. I vaulted into the stall, tackled his head, shot the intravenous dose in as fast as I could. We rolled him onto his back and wedged him into place with some hay bales. The intestines had now spilled onto the ground and were coated with straw.

I ran back to the truck and grabbed a bottle of sterile saline and some sterile towels. Gloving up, I gently lifted the loops of intestine and the owner poured a steady flow of saline, washing the dirt and straw away. I laid the cleaned loops onto the sterile towels, and had her hoist the towel as I began to frantically feed the intestines back into the scrotum.

Trying to shove six to eight feet of intestine into a small incision through a scrotum is extremely frustrating. It is like trying to shove an angry octopus into a Kleenex box. Loops of hypermotile bowel streamed around my frantic hands as I pushed with all of my force, trying to will everything to go back in where it belonged and praying it was staying fairly clean. At one point, I had the owner hold everything in place while I re-dosed the horse, hoping to stop him from straining.

After what felt like fifteen years, I had everything back into the abdomen and was preparing to suture the entire scrotum shut. As I was completely unprepared to perform an inguinal hernia repair in the field, the best I could do was patch him up and get him into the hospital. I ran a row of towel clamps up each incision to hold everything in until I could start suturing.

The owner had been silent throughout the mayhem, but finally she spoke.

"How much is all this going to cost?"

I looked at her. "The hernia repair will probably be at least two thousand dollars, give or take."

"Plus the cost of the castration?"

I nodded. "And some extra for the complications." Although it was hard not to feel responsible for the intestinal prolapse, the reality was that it was not my fault. It is a rare occurrence but can happen after a routine castration, and every seasoned vet I knew had seen it happen at least once. It was simply my turn.

The owner shook her head slowly. "Doc, I couldn't really afford to have you do the castrations today. I mean, I'll get you paid and everything, but I can't afford to take him in and get this fixed! I don't have two thousand dollars! Can't you just sew him up here?"

I explained that leaving a sutured scrotum full of active bowel wasn't fixing anything and it was a torsion or worse waiting to happen. The pony needed surgery to close the large inguinal ring, the portion of his abdomen that was communicating with the scrotum. It was most likely a congenital defect that had gone undetected.

"Put him down," she said finally, tears in her eyes.

I couldn't argue. Silently, I drew up the pink euthanasia solution and injected it into the vein, still seeing his kind gaze from earlier. The pony took a few deep breaths, shuddered once and was still, the friendly brown eyes still half open. I removed my clamps, and placed a quick suture to keep the intestines in while they dragged him off.

He was lying in his dim stall when I left, still propped up by the hay bales. The owner had gone into the house and the torn screen door banged gently in the midday breeze. The sky had clouded over, throwing a grim light on the buildings. I climbed into my truck and started the engine.

The place looked as desolate as I felt.

# The Legend of Excalibur

Spring work, the mainstay of any equine vet, comes in a rush. When the weather warms up, everyone remembers that they have horses, and the vets who have been playing checkers all winter are suddenly hustled off their feet. Horses need "spring shots," a medley of annual vaccines pertinent to geographical region and intended use of the horse. The geriatric in a closed herd will be vaccinated differently than the show horse with a busy season ahead.

The horses receive annual to biannual checkups, teeth are checked, shots given and dewormers discussed. If the teeth need attention, the horse is sedated, a mouth speculum placed, and the teeth are "floated," which means that sharp points are filed down and other dental abnormalities are identified and corrected. As horse's teeth erupt about 4 millimeters annually, it is necessary to perform regular dental exams to make sure all is well.

Typically when the horse is already sedated for the dental, the owner will request a sheath cleaning, or as one unforgettable client described it, "a hygiene." The horse is gifted with a retractable penis, and the tunnel that conceals the male equine reproductive organ is referred to as the sheath.

Gelded horses need to have their sheaths and penises cleaned semi-regularly; a task that tends to generate a stream of genital jokes and snickers from any passersby as they watch the vet bent double and scrubbing the horse's privates with green glop comically named "Excalibur." While some owners will perform this task themselves, many prefer to leave it to the vet.

In the tip of the equine penis is a blind ended pouch called the urethral diverticulum. Oils and other secretions can collect in this area, and over time will harden and get bigger and bigger, causing discomfort to the horse. It has to be manually removed, and woe to the ungloved, as your hands will stink for days. George once quipped, "Keeps you from biting your fingernails!"

The resulting greasy lump is referred to as a "bean," but many owners have trouble remembering that. An old man requested that I check for a "peanut" once, and several ladies have asked if I could be sure to remove the "pearl." A little British boy once watched me struggling to remove a bean and scrub a sheath for almost five minutes before asking, "Why are you washing his willy?"

The skin folds of the sheath also will get very dirty and require washing. I'm never sure if it is more fun to smell like horse sheath for the remainder of the day or to put myself into close proximity to the hind feet, which often whistle past me as the horse expresses his distaste for my gropings.

Some horses will "drop" for a cleaning, meaning they let the penis dangle so I can clean it. More commonly I'm chasing it into the sheath as it retreats for dear life, and my gloves are rendered useless as I'm buried to my elbow trying to fight the uncooperative Johnson back to daylight.

While the horse owner usually won't perform this task herself, she doesn't hesitate to supervise and point out crusty bits that you might have missed. Bent over, I'll have one arm draped over the horse's back, the other inside the sheath scrubbing away, and inevitably this is the position I'm in when a prospective owner is touring a boarding facility, trying to decide if they want to buy a horse for their little Anastasia. While offering to shake hands is an entertaining concept, instead I'll offer an upside down smile and keep washing.

My favorite sheath story centers around a horse named Slick. The call came in at 7 pm, on my birthday.

"Doc, gosh I hate to bug you, but I'm worried about my horse. I don't know what's wrong with him!"

I glanced out the window at my birthday party, now going on without me. "What seems to be the problem?"

"He's wringing his tail and he won't get out of the creek!"

This made no sense. "Is he lame?" I asked, thinking maybe he'd injured a leg.

"No! And he ate dinner just fine. He's not laying down, not rolling, but he does kick at his belly now and then."

I had the owner pull Slick out of the creek and check his vitals. Everything was normal, and the horse ate more hay when it was offered. This wasn't adding up at all.

"Doc, I think he'll be OK until the morning. Can you come up first thing?"

I could and was relieved to return to my party. The following morning, I made the 45-minute drive to the ranch, where the horse was waiting. He was back in the creek wringing his tail and occasionally kicking at his belly.

We coaxed him out and I checked him over thoroughly, even performing a rectal exam and inspecting his tail. His lower belly had a number of insect bites over it, but they did not seem to bother him. I tubed him with electrolytes and oil and just in case, gave him a dose of an anti-inflammatory medicine that was commonly used for belly pain.

Slick waited until I was finished, then marched back to the

creek, waded into it and continued wringing his tail. I was stumped.

George had told me a story once about a horse in Texas who was staggering around as though drunk, and for almost an hour he'd struggled to figure out the problem. Finally he sat on a fence, asked the client to leave him be, and just watched the horse.

Eventually, he realized that the horse was twisting his head strangely, as though something was hurting his ears. George checked the ears and discovered hundreds of ticks embedded all the way into the ear canal and on the tympanic membrane or "eardrum." After laying the horse down under general anesthesia, he removed all of the ticks and the horse made a full recovery.

I could almost hear him saying, "Shut up and watch the horse!" So I sat. And I watched. And after a long while, I noticed that some flies were swarming around the horse's sheath. I looked more closely and saw several crawl in and disappear, and several more crawl out, launch, and fly away like bees leaving a hive.

It couldn't be. I yelled to the owner to pull Slick back out of the creek, and I grabbed some gloves from my truck, pulling on a rectal sleeve for good measure. I eased a few fingers into the sheath, and the horse almost went to the ground and kicked violently at me. After a stiff dose of tranquilizer, I tried again, and was able to get my hand into the area. There was an unusual amount of debris in the sheath, and I grabbed a handful and drew my arm free.

My hand and arm were alive with maggots and a foul smell assaulted my nostrils. I yelped and flung my hand, and maggots filled the air and peppered the ground all around us. The owner shrieked so loudly that the sedated horse came to life, and all three of us engaged in a tribal dance of horror for a few minutes. When I calmed down, I tried to reassure the distraught owner who was hyperventilating, tears in his eyes.

Well, someone had to re-enter the maggot sheath, and it wasn't going to be the owner. I filled a bucket with warm water and diluted tea tree oil and spent the next twenty minutes cleaning every inch of that rotten sheath. There were shallow open sores everywhere, and after I had removed all of the maggots, I applied a thick layer of antibiotic and steroid cream and coated the outside of the sheath with an insecticide.

Sometimes a nasty necrotic wound or even a tumor will attract maggot-laying flies, but I had found neither. The dirty sheath had encouraged the insects to lay their eggs, and it had become a maggot den. From that point on, the owner had me clean the sheath more frequently, and the insects never returned.

When I told George the story, he grinned at me. George firmly believed that one should never treat a horse without a diagnosis, and he didn't miss this opportunity to rub it in.

"Bet you're glad you tubed him with those electrolytes!"

# The Horses on the Mountain

Snowball and Tuesday were two unassuming pasture mates who lived near McCoy, Colorado. They had been patients of George's and when he was gone, I became the ranch veterinarian. It lay deep in a valley of mountains, an idyllic spot with a clear pond and tidy outbuildings, and the horses had the run of the place.

Snowball was a big horse, a Saddlebred mix, and he was the more fearful of the two. Tuesday was a little sorrel mare who kept an eye on Snowball and was generally the brains of the operation. I kept up on their vaccinations and dental work, and aside from Snowball panicking if he lost sight of Tuesday for an instant, they were lovely patients, and I considered their owners to be friends.

One afternoon, I got a call from the ranch.

"Doc, Snowball was missing all night! We finally found him, but he's way up the mountain and won't come down. I don't think he can walk!"

"I'm on my way!" I said, turning the truck around. "On the way" meant I'd be there in 90 minutes, a frustrating timespan when an injured horse needs help. I probably broke a few laws getting there, but I made good time and the ranchers waited for me in a four-wheeler. As I drove through the gates, they took off up a rutted jeep track, beckoning me to follow.

45

We drove up the narrow road for probably 15 minutes, easing around the hairpin turns at each switchback. I cringed every time I rolled over a deep rut, trying not to picture the chaos happening inside the vet unit. But despite the worry clouding the journey, I couldn't help but admire the high green peaks, aspens all around me just beginning to turn gold. I'd been past the ranch hundreds of times but had never seen it from this angle and it was breathtaking. The air was fresh and cool and I inhaled it like an elixir.

I could see him in the distance, long before we reached him, Tuesday by his side. His huddled form stood in an open meadow about 50 feet from a small creek, and the grass was eaten down around him. His left forelimb hovered above the ground, a grotesque swelling evident at the point of the shoulder, and his body shivered, eyes half closed against the pain.

I was out of the truck before it stopped moving and quickly checked his vitals. High heart rate, moderate fever, gums brick red and congested with a slow refill time. There were gut sounds present, but they were diminished. The left shoulder was hard and hot, and I saw what looked like a puncture wound on the point of the shoulder draining some foamy yellow fluid. As I ran my hands over his trembling body, I noticed that the hard swelling extended under the shoulder, then along the ribcage, where I could palpate the crepitus and grinding of fractured ribs.

Gunshot injury. There was no other force that could have done this to this poor horse. Hunting season had begun, but it was black powder rifle and bow and arrow only. This injury had been inflicted by a high-powered rifle and the horse did not resemble an elk in the slightest. Who had done this and why?

I studied the surrounding mountains, so peaceful and sweet moments ago, now malignant with concealed rifle scopes. The trajectory of the puncture was directed upward, so whoever had shot had been downhill of the horse. And from the look of it, he'd been in open space, probably grazing happily with his buddy when the bullet hit.

I wanted to flood him with pain medicine, but knew that he was in shock and dehydrated, and I didn't dare give him medicine that could harm his kidneys until I had him stabilized. I placed a large-bore jugular catheter and hooked up a 5-liter bag of IV fluids. A horse this shocky needed at least 20 liters running at full speed, but we were out in the open with no place to hang up the bags, so we had to do them one at a time, taking turns holding them high in the air.

After 10 liters had gone in, he was brightening up considerably, and cautiously I injected a few drugs to help ease his pain. I had an AC converter wired into the vet truck, so I plugged in the clippers, shaved the injured area, and did what I could to clean and flush the deep bullet wound with dilute Betadine solution.

The ranchers had brought up some large ice packs and were holding them against the horse's shoulder and side, which he seemed to appreciate. Tuesday stayed close, pressing against her owners and Snowball. He was looking more alert and his head was resting on his owner's shoulder as she adjusted the cold packs on his body. Tears stood in her eyes as she murmured to him.

"Why would someone do this to you? Why! What the hell is wrong with people!"

By now, I could hear the ranch trailer clanking up the narrow road. Snowball hadn't been in a trailer for 15 years, but now he must load and endure the bouncy ride down to the barn. They brought the trailer right up to him, and his ears flickered nervously as he looked around for Tuesday, who had fled at the sound of the vehicles. He called to her, and she poked her head from behind a grove of aspens, studied the situation, then decided to return to her friend.

It took hours to get Snowball in the trailer. I had to leave and finish the rest of my calls, but the ranchers brought him down later that evening and stowed him safely in the barn, Tuesday by his side. I had left a lot of different medicines and a detailed treatment sheet, and cautioned them about him not surviving the night. I would be back the next morning to work on him again if he was still with us. I had offered referral to a hospital for more advanced care, but the owners declined. Either we'd fix him on the ranch, or he'd die on the ranch.

Cases like this had to be handled one day at a time. Earlier in my career, I'd try to spell out every possible outcome to the owners, and try to make predictions about what I thought the horse would do. After wasting words and breath, confusing the clients, and being wrong, a lot, I'd learned to shut up and just take the case as it progressed.

Snowball was still alive the following morning, but I was appalled to see the enormous amount of ventral edema on his belly and legs. He looked grotesque, a cartoon character of a horse. I could only speculate that the massive internal trauma had generated the fluid that was pooling in his subcutaneous tissues. His heart rate was still high and his gums were a frightening mottled pink and purple. His pulses in his lower limbs were normal, and he did want to eat, and reassuringly, his chest was clear.

I ran more fluids, gave more drugs, Tuesday looking anxiously over the stall partition. Snowball was on three different antibiotics, a medicine for pain and to prevent endotoxemia, and medicine to protect his stomach. The catheter was working fine, and there was a vet tech living on the property who had offered to do all of Snowball's treatments. I flushed the bullet wound again and again with my Betadine solution and applied a poultice over the injured tissues on his body.

I was working on his shoulder wound when I felt his warm breath on the small of my back where my shirt had pulled free. He pressed his muzzle into my skin and stayed there while I worked. When I'd finished and looked up at him, his soft brown eyes looked at me calmly, his head turned toward me, and suddenly I knew that we were going to get him through this no matter what it took. Some horses just want to live, and Snowball was one of them.

His recovery took almost two months. The horrible edema took a long time to go down, but gradually it did, and he never developed the complications I'd feared: laminitis, colic, pneumonia, sepsis. He remained calm and we started hand walking him for short distances on the second week, noticing that as he walked, he pumped out a great deal of foul smelling fluid and debris from the wound on his shoulder. I drained a massive seroma over the base of his ribcage at the two-week mark, and brownish watery fluid, fibrin clots and fragments of bone flowed from the incision I'd made. The ribs were starting to heal, and I wasn't keen on laying him down and trying to dig out the bone fragments, so I left things as they were.

Tuesday stayed close by Snowball throughout his recovery, and every time I drove past the ranch, I'd see them together, venturing farther and farther up the mountain. When I came to do their spring shots, both horses were happy and healthy, and aside from a rippled depression on Snowball's rib cage and a small scar at the shoulder, little evidence remained of his horrible injuries. The shoulder was a little stiff at the walk, but when Snowball broke into a run, there was no lameness evident.

A year passed, and as the leaves turned gold again, I was reminded of our group, high on the mountain, holding up Snowball's IV fluids and wondering if he'd survive. Every time I passed the ranch, I'd wonder who had shot the horse and why. I'd look for their sorrel and brown bodies, sometimes seeing them, sometimes not. The mountains in that area still seemed ominous. I always felt unseen eyes from the dark trees as I drove past and I'd whisper a prayer for the horses' safety.

It was spring when I ran into one of the people who'd helped save Snowball. She was an Animal Control Officer and lived on the ranch with the horses. She looked solemnly at me as she pulled out her iPhone and tapped up a photograph.

I studied it, unsure what I was seeing. It appeared to be a skeleton of a horse with some hide still attached. Sorrel hide. She reached over my shoulder and enlarged the picture. There was a hole blown through one of the vertebra of the neck. A bullet hole.

"Tuesday," she said, taking her phone back, her expression grim.

I stared at her, open mouthed. I couldn't say a word.

She told me that they now knew who had done this awful thing. It was a neighbor from an adjoining ranch who'd decided to invite some city friends up to shoot some bears. He'd decided that a horse carcass would make splendid bear bait.

"Can you press charges?" I asked.

She shrugged. "We have to prove he did it. Someone who knows the guy told us about it but he denied everything when we questioned him. If I can find the bullet that killed the horse, we can match it to his gun. That's about all we have."

I drove away, discouraged, remembering the long hours with Snowball and his long recovery. I remembered the tears on his owner's face, the naked hope in their eyes every time he showed improvement. And most of all, I remembered kind little Tuesday, that wouldn't leave his side.

Snowball was moved to a ranch where people didn't shoot horses for bear bait, and I haven't seen him since. His owners remain on the same ranch, and I still drive by often and automatically look for the brown and sorrel bodies of Snowball and his buddy Tuesday, wandering around together on their mountain.

# BREEDING HORSES

# Inbreeding

Client: *"I doubt the mare's pregnant, Doc. The only stud around'd be her son, and I can't see that happening!"*

*I raise my eyebrows but remain quiet. The man continues.*

*"And besides, that colt's too dumb to know what to do. He used to nurse the wall, that's how dumb he is!"*

*I palpate the mare. She is indeed pregnant, and I break the news to the client. He ponders my words, then breaks into a happy grin.*

*"They're a good bloodline, Doc! That foal'll be worth a lot of money!"*

# Twins

I was checking the last mare of the day and my arm was a noodle. Thanks to George, I enjoyed repro, and today I had been checking all of the mares on a big ranch for pregnancy. They had been relatively cooperative, but were big and strong and had squeezed the life from my right arm. I typically didn't have stocks to restrain the mares on the farm, so would park them half in, half out of the stall with their hindquarters in the aisle. The last mare was not interested in the stall, the barn aisle, or me, and it was a fiasco trying to get her checked.

I was using my ultrasound to rectally scan the uteruses. Some of the mares were newly bred, and accuracy was important. The last mare was throwing me around with my arm still inside her, aiming kicks at everything, and I was getting frustrated. I had glimpsed a pregnancy on the ultrasound screen, and it was tempting to just pronounce her pregnant and be done for the day. I usually liked to scan the uterus completely and be certain that only a single pregnancy existed, but this mare was so hateful that I just wanted to get away from her.

Fortunately, I didn't give up. I pulled my arm out, removed my rectal sleeve and went to the truck to get drugs to sedate her. I also had the staff put a twitch on her upper lip. When she was quiet, I slid my arm and the probe back inside and quickly located the uterus and the pregnancy. The remainder of the uterus was normal and I didn't see any additional fluid or suspicious-looking structures, but as I scanned back and forth over the vesicle, it became clear that she had a twin pregnancy, two vesicles on top of each other.

Twins in the mare are unwelcome news. There are reports of mares successfully carrying twins, and delivering them live, but this is rare and it is a very risky situation. More typically, one or both twins die in utero. The mare's health can be jeopardized also. The uterus of the mare is not designed to support twin pregnancies and can rupture during delivery. If the twins do survive, they are usually stunted and sickly.

I gave the mare a shot that would abort the pregnancy. There was nothing else I could do. If you catch a twin pregnancy early enough, sometimes you can pinch one of the vesicles, resulting in a single pregnancy, but she was too far along for this. By the size of the vesicles, it would be too late to get her back into heat and we'd have to wait until next season.

The clients were understanding, knowing that twins were not a good situation. But not everyone was this educated. I flashed back to another twin pregnancy that I had attended years before.

The caller was not someone I knew.

"Doctor, our mare just foaled. How quickly can you get here?"

I asked if mare and foal were OK and received an affirmative reply. The ranch was an hour away, and I had other calls lined up. I tried to educate the client and explain what to look for, trying to figure out how to fit them into my overbooked day.

Then: "Oh no! I think one of the foals just died! He's not breathing, Doctor!"

"I'm sorry, foals? Were there two babies born?"

"Yes. Isn't that normal?"

"I'm on my way!" I rushed to the truck.

When I arrived, the dead foal was laid in the back of the pickup, the mare calmly munching hay nearby. The other foal was curled in the straw. She was fairly normal on exam, although small, and she was able to stand and nurse without help. Reaching the udder was a bit of a struggle for her, but she managed, her milky little muzzle extended as far as it could reach. When I palpated her ribcage and abdomen, she gave a deep grunt that usually signified a full belly. All was well with her.

The mare was also typical for a postpartum exam. The vulva was intact, and there was just a small amount of bruising present. She had a full udder and both placentas had passed completely. I laid them out and checked for any abnormalities, but all seemed normal. The mare's vitals were normal and she was bright and alert, showing a healthy interest in the foal.

I inspected the dead foal. As first glance, it looked like a healthy, well-formed baby. Then I looked at the head. The forehead was grossly misshapen, bulging bizarrely from the eye sockets. The eyes were miniscule and the jaws were also deformed, barely protruding from the skull. The condition was called hydrocephalus, otherwise known as water on the brain. He'd had no chance of survival.

"This foal was alive when it was born?" I asked incredulously.

"Yes. He lifted his head and even seemed to struggle to get up at first. But right before he died, he made some awful sounds!"

I thought about asking her if she'd noticed the deformity of the head, but she seemed distressed so I let it go.

I asked the clients if I could have the head, and after looking at me strangely, they consented. I quickly decapitated the foal and put the dripping structure into a bucket to look at later.

Unfortunately, I forgot about the head when I pulled up to my next call, and a horse owner looked into the bucket as I was drawing up vaccines.

"What in God's name is that!" she shrieked.

"Um, it's a rare birth defect. I'm going to dissect it later." I tried, smiling broadly.

She looked at me. "Dr. Diehl, please don't take this personally, but you have a very strange job."

As I drove away, bulging head sloshing in the bucket, I realized that I really couldn't dispute that.

# Artificial Insemination

There weren't a lot of people breeding horses as the economy worsened. The market was terrible, and you could buy a pregnant mare with a foal by her side for $500. But I still had a few clients who were in the business and their breeding programs continued full speed.

Many times, a mare owner selects a stallion to breed to that lives in another state. In the Thoroughbred industry, the mare must travel to the stallion and be bred live, as any sort of artificial breeding is prohibited and the resulting foal would be unregisterable. Having said this, Thoroughbred mares are bred artificially all the time. As long as nobody "knows" this officially, all is well.

Other breeds don't have these restrictions, and semen can be collected from the stallion and tested. If it is good quality it can be extended with certain additives that allow a single collection to be divided into multiple doses. These doses are cooled, packaged and shipped all over the country to the waiting mares. Not all stallions extend and ship well, and a dose that initially had a high sperm count can drop by 40-60% over 24 hours. The longer a dose sits in the cooler, the more sperm cells die. So ideally the mare is bred as soon as the shipment arrives.

This means that the mares have to be followed closely and

the semen isn't ordered until the mare will be breedable. When you live far away from the stallion and you don't get Saturday or Sunday shipments, and the stallion is only collected on specific days, this increases the challenge of the timing.

We use certain hormones to help manage the mare's cycle, and can speed ovulation along as needed. It is easier to push a mare than to slow her down, and many a mare has ovulated before the semen arrives. If someone could invent a drug that would block ovulation for a set amount of time, there would be a huge market for it.

If you are using frozen semen to breed the mares, your timing has to be even more precise, ideally within 4-6 hours of ovulation. The mare should be in a facility to allow the vet to check her, sometimes every hour until she is ready to breed. The frozen semen will have already arrived and waits in a special nitrogen tank to keep it frozen until needed.

Field vets all have had their share of breeding disasters, and they cause premature gray hair. There is nothing as stressful as juggling the timing of the mare, the stallion, the mail, and the fantasies of the owner, not to mention the typical cost of getting a mare bred. And when things go wrong, they go really wrong.

I remember one farm that bred Warmbloods, and all of the mares were artificially inseminated, so I was there a lot. There were numerous farm dogs there that went around in a pack, and they were constantly underfoot when I was trying to work. My truck door bore long scratches from their claws, and when I went to and fro lugging equipment and getting out medicines, I'd trip over dogs, step on dogs, and endure dog noses goosing me in inappropriate places. I always had muddy pawprints all over my pants.

I'd asked the owner repeatedly to please put up the dogs. Sometimes she would, but more commonly they were everywhere. I tried to lock them in a stall once, but the barking was worse than tripping over them, so I had to let them out again.

I made the mistake of leaving my truck door open once as I was going back and forth hauling equipment, and a dog got into the cab and ate every bit of my lunch, tracking mud everywhere. The owner was placid when I complained, and told me that I shouldn't leave my door open.

Another time, a dog grabbed a bottle of expensive vaccine, chewing it to shreds. I was told gently that I just shouldn't leave things where the dogs could reach them. As the client was a nice lady other than the blind spot where the dogs were concerned, I gritted my teeth and tolerated the pack.

I had been working on one mare in particular that was proving very difficult to breed and had frustrated me for the last three cycles. Her uterus kept filling up with fluid after insemination, and despite flushing her repeatedly, she just wouldn't hold onto a pregnancy. The owner was able to talk the stallion owner into giving us one last chance with her, and it would be the last attempt of the season. I labored to get her clean and ready to breed one last time, and when the uterine cultures came back negative, I knew we could proceed.

I timed her pretty well, and when the semen arrived, she was ready to breed. I washed her carefully and bagged her tail, and the owner opened up the semen container and got everything ready. The dogs were more annoying than usual, and I kept kicking them away from my clean wash bucket as they tried to drink from it.

I slid on my sterile sleeve, squeezed sterile lube onto my arm, and opened the sterile pipette that we would use to deliver the semen directly into the uterus. Without looking, I held out my hand for the syringe of cooled semen that the owner normally had ready for me so I could charge the pipette before threading it into the mare. My hand stayed empty and I turned to see the owner looking frantically through the supplies on the table.

"Where did the baggie with the semen go? I laid it down right here!"

As she was speaking, I noticed one of the dogs dart past

me with an object in its mouth, the other dogs in hot pursuit. Before either of us could react, white liquid poured from the dog's mouth and was quickly lapped up by the pack. Just as quickly they left the barn, leaving the torn and empty baggie on the floor.

There wasn't much to say, although I thought of a few kind and gentle remarks about not leaving things where the dogs could get them. I packed up my gear in silence and loaded the truck, the owner sitting forlornly on a straw bale staring at her dogs. I knew how much this breeding had meant to her, and I couldn't wait to see the wretched dog pack finally disciplined.

As I opened my truck door, I heard her addressing the pack. "Now I am very, very disappointed in all of you ..."

# Breeding with Frozen

Another breeding drama involved an ill-mannered Thoroughbred mare that was so difficult to check that I had to sedate her every time I touched her. She'd lost her first pregnancy very early, and I still had time to try again before the season ended. I was able to check her daily, and everything was perfect when I ordered semen Thursday morning. It arrived on time on Friday, and I sedated her, washed her and bagged her tail.

I had a crowd of curious onlookers but no assistant, and I cut the zip tie on the blue shipping container holding the cooled semen, noticing that the clear tape, which usually was wrapped around the top, was missing. Every farm packaged semen a little differently, so I wasn't too worried. I lifted the lid, then realized that the metal cup which was supposed to hold the baggie of semen had been jammed in upside down. I worked it free, and realized that it was empty. There was no little baggie anywhere!

I turned the whole container upside down and shook it. Nothing. I checked the cup again. Nothing. The owner was in the stall with the mare, smiling happily, and I had to tell her that the lab had sent us an empty semen container. She thought I was kidding at first.

Phone calls to the lab were not helpful. They insisted that

they had sent us a full container and that the semen must have gotten stolen along the way. I tried to envision someone stealing a cold baggie of horse semen but just couldn't see it.

After a lot of back and forth, we learned that getting another shipment of cooled semen was impossible, as the stallion was several hours from the collection facility. They offered to send us some of his frozen semen instead.

I wrung my hands. Breeding with frozen was fine if we were still ahead of the mare, meaning we could get her bred right before ovulation. But she was so close, I knew she was going to ovulate that night, and it wasn't recommended to breed post ovulation with frozen semen.

We had no choice. We agreed to the frozen semen, and it arrived on a special Saturday shipment. Gloomily, I sedated the mare and checked her, and sure enough, she'd ovulated, a large spongy swelling where the follicle had been on her ovary. I thawed the semen and bred her anyway, knowing it was pointless.

Of course, when I checked her two weeks later, she was pregnant. Adding to the fun, she went on to develop late-term placentitis and other complications, and in a stunning grand finale, retained part of her placenta after foaling. The foal was crooked and bizarre looking, and even now, almost three years later, he resembles a mule more than the grand stallion that supposedly sired him.

# Long Distance AI

My most memorable breeding disaster happened early in my career. I was asked to breed two quarter horse mares to different reining stallions. The mares lived on a farm that was an hour drive from my house, and it would be very difficult to check them as often as I liked. I suggested that they just buy a proven horse, as neither mare showed any reining talent, but they wanted to breed reiners and that was that.

The owner was not involved in the horse care. Her son wanted the mares bred, and the property manager would be my assistant. When I arrived to check the mares for the first time, they were turned out in a large paddock, and the manager leaned on the fence, watching me expectantly, no halters in sight.

I never can understand what people expect me to do with loose horses. I have been escorted right up to the horse in the field, only to find that the owner has no halter. Or they have one in their hand, but I have to ask that they put it on so that I can examine the horse.

I explained how the process worked, and that the mares would need to be restrained in a stall so that I could safely rectal them and ultrasound their uteruses to determine the current stages of their ovulation cycles. I was told that the barn wasn't finished yet, and that there were no stalls.

We walked the property and finally found an area in the barn that I thought would work. I also would need electricity and a safe place to set up my ultrasound so that the mares couldn't knock it over.

Naturally the mares didn't want any part of being checked, and it was well over an hour before I was finished with them. One kept trying to kick me, and I finally had to sedate her.

Of course they were in completely different stages of their cycles. When you are breeding multiple animals on the same farm, ideally their cycles are doing similar things at similar times. This was going to be a little more challenging, but I had drugs that I could use to get them synched.

I short-cycled one mare, and let the other one go without drugs. Hopefully we'd be ordering semen at the same time when they were ready. I'd return in two days to check them, making sure that it would be in the beginning of the week so that we could give the stallion owners plenty of notice and that the mail would work to our advantage.

We turned the mares out and the manager was on the phone with the owner, updating her. After listening to his interpretation of what we'd just done, I figured that I'd better go talk to her myself.

She was on the phone when I arrived at her office, and I had to sit and wait. When she hung up, she announced that she'd just finished ordering the semen for both mares and it would be here tomorrow!

After a lot of discussion about how sperm were living cells that died when they sat around in a container, and that the mares weren't ready to breed yet, she gave me a disgusted look and cancelled the orders. I pictured the reaction of the stallion owners who had just realized what amateurs they were dealing with.

The recheck went a little better, but the mares were still far out in the field when I arrived and I had to wait an extra 20 minutes while the manager chased them in circles. I suggested that maybe he could have them caught and waiting for me next time, but this never did happen.

The mares were ready to breed when I checked them early Thursday morning, and I called the stallion managers myself and placed the orders. The stallions would be collected that morning and we'd breed the mares on Friday.

Everything went fine and I had both mares bred by Friday around lunchtime. They both ovulated on Saturday, which was ideal. I was dragging from all of the mileage I'd logged, and still had to explain to the owner that the mares weren't automatically pregnant, and we wouldn't know for another two weeks. This time I got rolled eyes and a loud sigh.

On the appointed day, I checked the mares. One was pregnant and the other was not. We went over the bill and I had to explain several times that even though the one mare was not pregnant, there were still considerable charges associated with the breeding, and there would be more charges for trying again. There are a percentage of owners who feel that our charges should be outcome based, and she was one of them. When I wouldn't budge on the bill, she decided not to re-breed the open mare.

The pregnant mare progressed normally. I'd been a little worried about breeding her, as she was 15 and a maiden, but she was strong and healthy. I checked her at Day 35 and could see a fetal heartbeat. Everything looked good at the 60- and 90-day checks. Her weight and condition were normal, and her pretty sorrel coat gleamed when she was in the sun. When I drove past the ranch I could see her grazing in the field, her round belly hanging low. We vaccinated her a month before foaling per the current protocols, and the last month of her pregnancy was uneventful.

I had spent a lot of time trying to educate the farm manager as to what to look for, as he'd probably be the one attending the foaling. He seemed to know more about heavy equipment than horses, but he was attentive to my lectures and I knew he'd do his best.

I always had an ear towards the phone when I had a mare getting close. The call came at 2:30 a.m. It was the owner.

"The foal is out, but the mare won't get up! It's like she's unconscious!"

I leaped out of bed. "Is she breathing?"

A pause. "No."

"Touch her eye! Does she blink?"

"No."

Shit! I flew around the room getting dressed. After giving the owner instructions to milk the mare to get the precious first milk, or colostrum, the life-giving fluid that was essential to the foal's survival, I sped out the door. I got pulled over driving to another farm to pick up some more frozen colostrum, and after a lot of explaining and apologies, the police let me go with a warning.

I raced to the farm, and arrived to a bloodbath. The mare, obviously dead, lay sprawled in the aisle, the foal wandering around helplessly among farm equipment and rolls of fencing. Blood was everywhere – on the walls, on the floor, with a dark red stream flowing down the center of the aisle. The family clutched each other and cried, and a neighbor was trying to milk the dead mare. The manager was pacing, frantic.

I cornered the foal and lifted him away from the fencing rolls. The neighbor helped me get him corralled in a safe area and we bedded it heavily with straw. I got a bucket of warm water and started slowly thawing the colostrum I'd brought. It can't be microwaved or heated too quickly or the proteins will be destroyed.

The foal was healthy and strong, just hungry, and the neighbor was able to bottle feed about three ounces of the mare's own colostrum. We'd need a lot more than that, and I anticipated feeding all of what I'd brought.

It was time to inspect the deceased mare and find out what had gone so terribly wrong. I lifted her lip and pulled down her eyelid and her conjunctiva and mucus membranes were gray white. When I lifted her bloody tail, I was stunned by the sight of her large colon protruding from her vulva. Further exam revealed a tear that split the long shelf of tissue that separates rectum from vulva, probably made by the foal's leg as the mare strained. The uterus had also ruptured. My arm mingled freely with the remainder of the contents of the abdomen.

I'd never seen a tear this extreme. The hemorrhage may have come from the large vessels of the colon or from the uterine arteries, but it didn't matter at this point. The foaling had destroyed this poor mare and even if she'd survived, she would have needed major surgery to repair the damage. For her sake, I was glad she was gone.

It was hard not to feel at fault. I still think about her and my early misgivings about breeding her. We can't be responsible for outcomes like this, but the fact was that I had bred the mare and she'd died horribly because of the foal. It haunted me for a long time.

The orphan foal was paired with a surrogate mare that had lost her own baby. The foal did well with the new mare, was weaned on time and returned to the original farm. He is now a full-grown horse that shows no talent for reining.

# CLIENTS: THE GOOD, THE BAD AND THE UGLY

*Me: "Hello, this is Dr Diehl, can I help you?"*
*Caller: "Uh. Hello?"*
*Me: "Yes? Dr Diehl speaking, can I help you?"*
*Caller: "Oh....I....well....Courtney?"*
*Me: "Can I help you with something?"*
*Caller: "Did I call a vet?"*
*Me: "Dr Diehl. Yes. What did you need?"*
*Caller: "A vet. Are you Courtney?"*
*Me: "That is my first name, yes. I'm sorry, who's calling?"*
*Caller: "Oh, you don't know me, Courtney. I just have a few questions about my pregnant mare, an old cut on a leg, and my feeding program. So to begin...."*
*Me: "Did you need a phone consult or do you just have a quick question? I'm actually with a client right now, so if this is going to take a while then I'd like to schedule..."*
*Caller: [Harsh sigh] "I guess you're too BUSY to talk to me, Courtney. I suppose we can talk when you have TIME!"*

*Me:  "Yes, I'm sorry, my day is pretty full.  May I call you this evening?"*

*Caller:  "Well, if that's the soonest you're available...."*

*Me:  "May I just get your name and number?"*

*Caller:  "That's Dr. Cara Elvin. I'm a psychologist. [provides telephone number]*

*Me: Great, Cara. I'll speak to you in a few hours then."*

*Caller: "That's DR Elvin.  I'll be expecting your call."*

# I have a show to get to!

*Client: "I just want you to know that this is a very expensive horse!"*

*Me: "OK."*

*Client: "Expensive. Like REALLY expensive. So I don't want any problems!"*

*Me: "Me neither."*

*Client: "I hope you are taking this seriously."*

*Me: "Absolutely."*

*Client: "Because the last vet didn't take this seriously."*

*Me: "How's that?"*

*Client: [in a hushed tone] "My horse goes lame sometimes."*

*Me: "OK ...?"*

*Client: "He can't go lame! I need to show him! You need to take this seriously! I'm not sure you're taking this seriously!"*

*Me: "What exactly would you like from me today?"*

*Client: "To keep my horse sound! The other vet said he needed several months off! Can you believe that?"*

*Me: "Was there a diagnosis?"*

*Client: "He said he'd hurt a ligament, I don't know."*

*Me: "Suspensory?"*

*Client: "That could be it. Yeah, that's what he said, I think."*

Me: "Those can take a long time to heal. Six to eight months!"

Client: "The horse is very expensive!"

Me: "And the expensive ones heal at the same speed as the cheap ones. You can't ride this horse with this injury!"

Client: [disgusted sigh] "What other vets do you recommend?"

Me: "How many have you called?"

Client: "You're the third."

Me: "I guess none of us are taking this seriously?"

Client: "This is a very expensive horse!"

# It's in the Shoulder, Doc!

*Me: "The lameness problem is in the foot. I found a large abscess in the heel."*

*Trainer: "Have you checked the shoulder? I saw the video, and it looks like shoulder to me!"*

*Me: "There's pus draining from the foot."*

*Trainer: "Because I know this horse really well, and I know how he moves when he's sore!"*

*Me: "Yes, well, you see ..."*

*Trainer: "I'm in Illinois right now, then I fly to Colorado. I'm going to check his shoulder when I get there!"*

*Me: "He'll probably be fine when you get here. These usually take about three days to resolve."*

*Trainer: "No. Shoulders take a lot longer than that to heal!"*

*Me: "Out of curiosity, what makes you think it's the shoulder?"*

*Trainer: "The last time he went lame, I had the vet inject his shoulder. It fixed him."*

*Me: "He'll probably be fine when you get here."*

*Trainer: "Then inject his shoulder before I get there! We've got to stay ahead of this thing!"*

# Trainers, Show People and Faith

When you practice equine medicine, you will eventually come up against the "show people" and their trainers, who manipulate them like demented puppet masters. Many times I have been explaining something to the owner of the horse, only to come face to face with a red faced, pop-eyed trainer, who lets me know in no uncertain terms that all medical discussions go through them first.

These trainers usually have more drugs in their trunks than I carry on my truck, all with mysterious names like "Arquel," "Serapin," or "Kentucky Red," and enough steroids and hormones to dope the entire Tour de France.

The lists of the "required medicines" that many show horses will have in their file is alarming, and usually have not been prescribed by a veterinarian. I have reviewed many of these lists, and will often discover that a horse is receiving two versions of the same drug, resulting in dangerous overdoses, as well as numerous unnecessary drugs for undiagnosed problems. Trying to educate the owners is fruitless, as science-based medicine is effortlessly overruled by the trainer who "knows" the horse better than we do, and "knows" what it takes to win ribbons.

In this environment, our job as veterinarian is to cheerfully refill prescriptions, inject joints on request, ask no questions, and agree with the trainers. When a trained monkey could perform your job as well as you, it's time to rethink some things.

I still hold onto hope that ethical vets can educate the show horse owners. I still make the mistake of assuming that good medicine, logic and controlled studies of efficacy can win out over the black magic witchery of the show and competition world. I'm fighting a losing battle. These next few chapters detail what my life was like in the company of some of these people, and how I preserved my sanity with prayer and faith. If I had not brought God into the equation, I might have ended up in the loony bin. Lord knows I was close.

It's no contest who the authority is within the horse's entourage. Hint: It's not likely to ever be the vet. If the trainer says it, it's gospel truth. If the trainer dictates that the horse needs his hocks "done," then they need to be injected, and if the horse performs poorly, it's my fault for not following directions and I am fired. If the trainer wants bleach injected into the jugular vein because it helps red cells carry more oxygen and makes the horse faster, woe to the vet who fails to agree. Ditto silicone injections into the joints, Viagra in feed, steroids under the tongue, and any other potion endorsed by the trainer.

I have stopped counting how many times I've been fired by trainers.

Most owners are so fearful of not being in the "know" that they will nod sagely when the trainer injects the substance of the day. Many more owners simply have no idea of what is being put into their horses, but wouldn't think to question the hefty bills that arrive like clockwork. It's all about the blue ribbons – if you're only going to bring home a white one, don't even bother.

I had several interactions with a trainer whom I shall refer to as "Eloise," and they typically left my head spinning. She was popular with the wealthy horse owners, and her dominant personality was overwhelming. Eloise got her way, period, and the owners who questioned her methods were out on their ear before they could turn around.

The myth of Eloise was far greater than her accomplishment list, but this disconnect didn't seem to register with the breathless riders who accepted her iron-fist rule without question. Eloise had the answers and could get the ribbons, and that was the end of the discussion.

I would see, or rather hear Eloise, as I made my rounds through a barn where we both had clients. Her piercing tones permeated every inch of the closed space, and it was very distracting to try to work up a sick horse with her vocal acrobatics vibrating your eardrums.

A favorite memory of Eloise is watching her shriek into a cell phone while long-lining a horse and rider in circles around her. She never moved a step, just lifted her arm over her head as the horse and helpless rider sailed around her, talking away the whole time.

Occasionally Eloise would hit me up for some drug or another, informing me that it wasn't for her, but "Mr. So and So," who would be very upset if it were not produced immediately. These veiled threats and associations with mighty people were supposed to make me genuflect in her direction, but I never came through for her. She had a vet, who we'll call Dr. Yesman, who would scoot to do her bidding as directed, so she didn't really need me, but she kept trying.

Fortunately most of my clients saw through her, so my interactions with her were limited, but one experience stands out in my mind for many reasons. It was not only the first truly challenging situation that I'd dealt with involving a trainer and a client, but also my first time bringing God into a tough situation that I could not handle on my own. I realize that God discussions are uncomfortable for some, and I hope my audience can read this story with an open mind and heart.

Achilles, an Irish Sport Horse, had been an elite eventer, and rumored to have been an Olympic hopeful. True or not, he was a stunning horse, and was gentle and kind as well. He was purchased for tens of thousands of dollars by a client of mine with the stipulation that he could "no longer jump, but was OK for flat work."

I was concerned that the owner had purchased the horse without a vet check, but she assured me that Eloise knew everything about the horse, and that was good enough for her. Eloise was not her trainer at the time, but had been pursuing her, and I was worried that she was starting to gain mental control.

Right from the start there was trouble. Eloise, eager for this opening with my client, presented her with a daily list of Achilles' required medications that would have sizzled the kidneys of the most seasoned drug addict. I read through the list with dismay, and realized that the next request would be for me to provide all of these drugs to keep the horse "sound."

Thinking I could win with logic and science, I requested the vet records on the horse, and a written diagnosis of the lameness that prevented jumping and the need for the medications. This request was shrugged off as unnecessary, and no records were forthcoming.

Eloise informed my client that Dr. Yesman would provide the medications for Achilles without discussion, as he respected Eloise's tremendous knowledge of the show horse. I ignored the intended implication that I, therefore, had no knowledge of the show horse, and stood my ground, something she wasn't used to. I explained that since I was a licensed veterinarian, not a trained monkey, I would not be handing over drugs without a medical diagnosis.

That did not go over well. The climate in the barn, already tense, changed from cold disdain to open warfare. Eloise would snicker loudly about my level of competency in my presence, approach my clients when I was working on their horses and question what I was doing, badmouth me behind my back, and generally do everything in her power to be toxic and foul. She had a small army of equally nasty women whom I hardly knew that would mirror her behavior toward me every chance they got. My heart sank every time I was called to the barn.

Some people listened to her and refused to call me for any vet work. I had some loyal clients who held fast, but several defected during this time and switched to Dr. Yesman, the "show" vet who understood what the horses "needed." Other clients started to question me openly, quoting Eloise as saying their horse could advance a whole level if we'd only start the maintenance joint injections as she recommended. I could usually get that one under control by asking the owners when they started their teenage kids on maintenance joint injections, but it was exhausting to constantly be questioned and mistrusted.

I was only a few years out of vet school, and it hurt to have people hate me so openly. All I was trying to do was practice the quality of medicine true to the way I had been trained. It was bad medicine to drug animals without a diagnosis, and I was not going to compromise on that.

I had a lot of moments behind the wheel of the vet truck when I put the invisible Eloise in her place and she would crawl to me begging for forgiveness, and promise to leave the horse world forever, never to be seen again. Drivers next to me probably thought I was insane, waving my arms and bellowing at an empty passenger seat. Worse, I found myself criticizing Eloise and her gang to clients, wanting to hurt them as much as they were hurting me.

Weeks passed, and my client continued to request the drugs for Achilles, who was not sound, and I continued to refuse to provide them without the vet records, which never appeared. I told her many times that we needed to do a lameness exam on Achilles, which she would think about and then refuse.

We were at a stalemate, and Eloise was now openly calling my client and telling her the harm I was doing to Achilles by not keeping him up on his medications. The situation was really getting to me. I felt unfairly attacked and poisoned by the ordeal, and I had no idea of what to do or how to handle it. Why wasn't logic and science enough?

It seemed like every time I opened my mouth, negative things about Eloise and the situation came out, and I was sinking into consuming resentment. It woke me at night and tormented me so that I could not fall back to sleep. In total desperation, I began to seek conscious contact with God, as no human entity was going to help me through this, and I literally could not take it anymore. I felt like I was going crazy.

When I look back on this story, I wonder why God is often the last resort for many of us experiencing a painful situation. Beginning to reach for God took me from complete desperation to a level of peaceful acceptance and patience that was missing from the equation. It was amazing how quickly the prayers started to help me.

I was saying multiple prayers a day for a resolution to the standoff, and for more patience and guidance without compromising my standards. I was waiting for the phone call from my client telling me that she had switched to Dr. Yesman and would no longer need my services, but one day she called and requested that I perform a lameness exam on Achilles! I had gotten through to her after all, and my prayers had clearly worked! Now everything would go my way, I thought.

I could hardly wait to get started. I arrived at the barn with everything I would need, and the barn manager, sympathetic to the situation, agreed to help out with the exam. We jogged Achilles on the cement breezeway in the barn, longed him in the dirt arena, had a rider hop on him and take him through some exercises.

Achilles had consistent right forelimb lameness at the trot, which got worse on the turns to the right. I couldn't see it at the walk. There was no swelling or pain to palpation, and flexion tests did not seem to change the lameness much.

Eloise had insisted that her Natural shoer who did all of the show horses be the one to shoe Achilles, so I had to pull off a square-toed aluminum shoe with a thick plastic pad before I could put hoof testers on him. There was little pain response in the foot to the testers except for a moderate soreness over the center of the frog.

When the cause of lameness is not obvious after the exam, vets are taught to perform diagnostic nerve blocks to find the area of pain. We systematically inject local anesthetic into specific areas of the leg, starting with the heel and slowly working our way up until the horse goes sound.

The blocks don't tell us why the horse is hurting, but they tell us the location of the pain in the leg. Then we know where to take our X-rays and focus our other diagnostics. I discussed this with my client and she agreed to let me start nerve-blocking Achilles.

By now, we had a small audience around us – a common occurrence for any vet in a barn. Vet work of any kind is often the barn entertainment, and privacy goes out the window as other horse owners saunter over and start asking questions as though the horse were theirs. They park themselves in chairs, sit on the arena wall, lean against the back of the vet unit where I am trying to work, and enjoy the show. If there's a good way to scatter a nosey audience in a barn, I have not yet discovered it. I did draw the line at a woman who started poking through the drawers of my vet unit.

I lifted Achilles' front leg, and scrubbed the area where I would be injecting the first amount of lidocaine. He behaved perfectly for the injections to temporarily numb the nerves to the right heel. I let the leg down and set the timer on my watch. We would watch him go at five minutes, then at ten. At this point in the lameness exam, you never knew if you were in for a long day of blocking or if the first block would locate the problem.

The observers assumed I was finally injecting Achilles with magic drugs that would cure the lameness, and were noisy in their approval when he jogged off sound at five minutes. Finally

I had joined the ranks of the larger-than-life Dr. Yesman, a vet who could cure in one visit! I figured it would be a waste of time to try to educate the crowd. Clearly patient confidentiality wasn't an issue either.

To be thorough, I watched Achilles again at ten minutes, and when he was still sound, began to set up the X-ray (radiograph) equipment. Although I knew where the pain was coming from, I still didn't know why the pain was there, so it was time to look further.

The radiographs would show a picture of the bones and some limited views of soft tissue structures, and I always felt fortunate to find my diagnosis there – a bone chip, changes to the bone structure or density, fluid around a tendon, arthritis, etc. If the images were clean or inconclusive, it didn't mean that we had the wrong area, just that further soft tissue imaging like ultrasound or MRI were necessary to try to find out the reason for the lameness.

Some clients appreciated this logical approach. Others questioned why I didn't immediately know what was wrong with the horse and how to fix it. Dr. Yesman didn't waste time with all of this. He could just glance at the horse and offer a diagnosis and a treatment, usually involving steroids and joint injections.

Eloise was there, informing the owner that the X-rays weren't necessary and would be costly. The owner seemed to be listening to her and turned apologetically to me, but surprisingly the barn manager stepped in. She was no fan of Eloise either, but had kept the peace over the last few months.

Now, apparently, she had had enough. She informed the owner that we were working up Achilles properly and it was overdue. Her defense of me was unexpected and thorough. I focused on setting up my equipment, overwhelmed at having her support. She kindly offered to hold the X-ray plates while we took the pictures.

The X-rays were good quality but unfortunately, there was

no obvious cause for Achilles' lameness. There were several abnormalities that concerned me as I studied each image carefully. The crowd of onlookers was back, Eloise among them, and I wished I'd been able to come up with a final diagnosis on this high-visibility case but it wasn't to be. I needed to do more diagnostics and would return in a few days.

As the crowd cleared out, one lady remarked that she'd never seen Dr. Yesman cure a lameness as quickly as I just had. I sighed as I packed the truck. Tomorrow, when the nerve block wore off completely, Achilles would return to the same level of lameness, and I would return to the same level of idiot incompetency. I couldn't win.

I made sure to tell the owner that Achilles needed full rest until the diagnosis was completed. Maybe no one would notice when he started limping again.

I held off on sending the radiographs to a specialist right away, as I wanted to perform a separate block when I was sure that the first one had worn off totally. The first block that I had done numbed the heels and also the lowest joint in the leg. I wanted to block that joint separately to see if it might be the cause of the pain, as treating the affected joint was something I could do on the farm.

The barn manager and I did the joint block early morning the following week. No one was around to comment on the fact the Achilles was lame "again" and that my joint block didn't cure him this time. I felt satisfied by the results, knowing that injecting this joint with any medication would be a waste of time and money.

Although I still didn't know what the problem was, I had a lot more information about what it was not. It was time for an MRI to take a closer look at the ligaments and tendons in the heel region. For this, Achilles would have to be hauled to a large equine hospital more than three hours away.

Eloise lost no time in telling the barn that I had no idea what was wrong with Achilles, who was now lame again, as my injection had failed, and that I now had to bring in another vet to diagnose him. She ranted loudly about Dr. Yesman not being allowed to look at him, and this time the owner seemed to be listening to her. I was trying to press the long trip to the hospital, and several thousand dollars in diagnostics, and Eloise was offering her a cheap trip to soundness.

Eloise won.

I arrived at the barn one morning to find Dr. Yesman bent over Achilles' front leg, injecting something into the lowest joint in his leg – the same joint I had blocked with no improvement. Eloise crouched by his side, passing him syringes. The owner had her back to me, but the barn manager was there holding Achilles and made eye contact with me. She grimaced apologetically. No one else acknowledged me.

I got through my calls, and left as soon as I could, resentment pounding at my temples. I thought I was on top of this situation! Damn it, I'd been praying and praying! How come God had let me down? The passenger seat of my truck took a vicious verbal beating, and I hollered out all of my frustration and rage at God and at another invisible Eloise, who seemed determined to ruin my career. I bent my steering wheel pounding on it. I went home and I prayed again for patience, for forgiveness. There was nothing else I could do.

I forced myself to pray for the ability to turn over my anger to God. I also prayed for Eloise and Dr. Yesman, although I did not want to. At first, the best I could do was mutter through clenched teeth for an abundance of God's will in their lives. It got easier over time, and it helped if I pictured them as small children who didn't know any better. As I kept at it, the resentment and hurt subsided, and no longer sprung into my head at random moments, taking control of my emotions.

Eventually I could think of them without rage, and I was even beginning to wish for true goodness to come into their lives. I felt more peace and grace coming into my life, and if I backslid into negative emotions, I would stop and pray again, sometimes numerous times a day, to release the negative feelings and replace them with forgiveness.

During this time it occurred to me that allowing negative emotions to dominate me not only caused me further misery, but also demonstrated an outward lack of faith in God's ability to take care of the situation. I started to realize that praying for things that I wanted to happen wasn't the right approach. Praying for God's presence and guidance was enough. My sense of peace strengthened even more as I consciously reached to God to help me through something that I could not solve on my own and trust that God's way was better than mine.

I would see Achilles over the next few weeks, laboring through his flat work, never comfortable. He wrung his tail, flung his head down to start a trot, and was still short-strided on the right front leg. He seemed to be getting worse. I saw medicines poured down his throat, injections pushed into his neck, supplements mixed into his feed. Dr. Yesman was a regular visitor to his stall, and I would often see him and Eloise in whispered conferences. The owner kept her distance from me, and I tried not to take it personally. Some days I succeeded.

Then one day the phone rang. It was the owner, telling me that she had decided to take Achilles in for the MRI. As though we had just spoken, I told her that I hoped we would be able to get a diagnosis and I wished her and Achilles a safe trip. I called the hospital and made sure they'd received all of my records and the X-rays.

One week later, I received a call from the clinician who had looked at Achilles. The MRI showed chronic damage to a big tendon that attached to the bottom of his pedal (foot) bone, and a large new tear in the same area. It was a very bad injury for a horse to have, and recovery would take months. We didn't know if he'd be able to return to any level of soundness.

Achilles was to stay at the hospital for treatment and eventually would return home for follow-up care. I was gratified to get another call from the owner, asking me if I would work with the clinicians from the big hospital and make sure Achilles got everything he needed. Eloise and Dr. Yesman were not mentioned.

Achilles spent more than three weeks at the hospital receiving stem cell injections into the area of the injury and came home with a special shoe to help the torn tendon heal. He remained on stall rest for a long time, then we started hand-walking him, gradually increased his exercise, then worked up to riding. He will never be a jumper again, but performs dressage beautifully and does well at shows without any medications. He has remained sound for several years.

Eloise kept her distance after the MRI, but continued to blame me for not providing the medications in the first place. I confronted her once, hoping for a resolution, but it did no good. Engaging with her is pointless. I am civil when I see her, and I rarely think of her otherwise.

When I look back on this story, I wonder why God is often the last resort for many of us experiencing a painful situation. It was amazing how quickly I was freed from consuming resentment just by asking for help. My prayers did not punish Eloise or make me the great vet who diagnosed the horse and fixed the problem, but they made me stronger and better in ways that were much more important.

# The Vaccine Reaction

*Client: "Doctor, my horse is having a vaccine reaction! I think you need to come right away!"*

*Me: "Gosh, it's been five days since the shots. That's strange. Can he breathe? Is he acting distressed?"*

*Client: "Yes! But he's eating right now, and I hate to interrupt him when he's eating!"*

*Me: "If he can eat, he can breathe. What seems to be the problem?"*

*Client: "He looks sad."*

*Me: "He looks sad?"*

*Client: "Yes. That and he's eating more slowly than normal."*

*Me: "That doesn't sound like a vaccine reaction to me."*

*Client: "Well he didn't do this last year!"*

*Me: "We didn't vaccinate him last year."*

*Client: "You see? Oh, I knew this would happen! Are you sure you gave the shots properly?"*

*Me: "Yes."*

*Client: "Because he kind of flinched when you gave them."*

*Me: "Have you ever gotten a shot? They do tend to hurt a little."*

*Client: "He's never flinched before! Oh, I'm so worried!"*

*Me: "OK, I'll come check him out if you like, but really, I think you're worrying unnecessarily! What time can you meet me today?"*

*Client: "Oh, I'm actually in Denver right now. My girlfriends are at the barn with him."*

# The 2 A.M. Phone Call

*Me: "I don't have you in my computer. Who is your regular vet?"*

*Random Person: "Well, these aren't my animals."*

*Me: "Right. Who is the owner?"*

*Random Person: "Well, one animal is owned by my friend. And the other is owned by another friend."*

*Me: "OK, but who is the regular vet for these animals?!"*

*Random Person: [Provides clinic name] "But they need cash up front before they'll see us!"*

*Me: "Well, I do as well."*

*Random Person: "Oh. Well, can you just tell me what to do over the phone, then?"*

# Moon Blindness

"Moon Blindness" is a common eye problem in horses and I saw quite a bit of it in practice. Thanks to the romantic name, there are clients who are certain that moonlight causes this disorder but there is no actual correlation between the moon and eye problems. The disease is thought to be caused by an autoimmune problem. It causes runny, painful eyes, and it is important to diagnose it properly so as not to treat it with medicine that could cause more harm.

I was treating one such case in an old Thoroughbred. The old guy was not particularly keen on vets, and had a habit of flinging his big head at me when I was trying to look at his eyes through my ophthalmoscope. The eyes had been getting worse lately, despite regular treatment, and I was dismayed to see a large ulcer on the left cornea. I squirted some special dye into the left eye, and more than half the cornea soaked up the green stain, indicating damage to the surface.

The medical term for this disease is Equine Recurrent Uveitis. Some of these cases reach an end stage where the eye shrinks and becomes full of scar tissue, and I feared this was where we were headed. Nothing I was doing was helping.

The owners were well-intended but tiring in their constant stream of questions. They usually followed the medication regimen to the letter, but my recheck visits usually took twice as long as they should due to the endless discussions covering everything horse-related.

I'd be squinting sadly into the eye, which steadily grew worse despite the medley of antibiotics, dilators and other medications being poured into it, and it would start.

"Doctor, don't you feel that his weight looks excellent right now? I'm feeding him a kelp extract along with ground seashells with some diatomaceous earth mixed in. My calculations show that this is addressing his calcium imbalance and stimulating his immune system. Do you agree?"

The wife would interject, "But he won't eat the powder the way you mix it in. I have to come back and add molasses and mix it in with the soaked beet pulp and ground flax seeds. It all just sits on the bottom otherwise."

"No, it's the beet pulp he won't eat. He likes the kelp flavor! I've seen him eating it."

"He won't even stay in the stall to eat the way he used to! I have to carry his buckets out to him in the field and he walks away from me. I think his coat looks dull. Don't you think his coat looks dull?"

"Yes, it does, and I noticed he's walking funny. Doctor, what do you think of his feet? I think his toes need to be shorter and I've discussed this with the farrier ..."

I held up a hand. "Right now, let's talk about the eye. It just isn't responding to the therapy like I had hoped."

The wife looked at her husband. "Did he let you put the drops in last night?"

"He was blinking a lot and it wasn't easy, but I got them in. I read that Vitamin C might stimulate healing. Maybe we should add that to his diet"

"Because he looked better yesterday, I thought. Maybe the drops didn't go in all the way!" insisted the wife.

"No, they went in! And the way he was holding his head

made me think his teeth were bothering him. Maybe we should check his teeth while you're here. Would you have time to float his teeth?"

I interrupted. "This isn't because of last night. This eye has been getting worse since my last visit. I think he's holding his head like that because of the pain, not the teeth. And I don't think it's anyone's fault."

And hopefully not mine, I thought. I'd been on the phone multiple times with an eye specialist and had emailed pictures and updates, but nothing seemed to be working. I had discussed installing a lavage kit into the eye to make administering the drops easier, but they insisted they could do them without the kit. The old horse was very cooperative with them despite the obvious pain he was in.

I studied him. The eye was almost completely closed, and tears stained the hair under his eye. The eye itself was getting softer and smaller, and there was no vision at all. Although I had hoped to be able to save the vision in the eye, we could live with a blind, quiet eye. A blind, painful eye would be a constant source of misery to the horse. If this were the case, I would need to surgically remove it.

I tried to explain this to the couple. The husband was thinking hard.

"I see. But he'll look weird with one eye."

"Yes, the empty eye socket can look strange, but I can put a silicon spacer in," I explained. "The lids are sewn shut over it, but it keeps the empty socket from sinking in."

"Oh perfect. Let's do that! Can we get one to match his other eye?"

"Well, you can't see the spacer. The lids are sewn closed over it."

"Well, if you do that, how can he see out of it?!" exclaimed the husband.

I kept quiet.

The wife looked at me, then at her husband, wide eyed.

Comprehension dawned on both simultaneously, and they began to laugh. I had to join them.

Naturally another 30-minute discussion ensued, but I was comforted knowing that the horse was getting excellent nursing care from two people who clearly adored him.

I never did have to remove the eye. The owners kept up with the treatments to prevent infection, and it eventually shrunk itself down into a painless ball of tissue, and bothered the horse no more.

# Little Big Dog

It was late evening on a weekday and I had just stepped out of the shower – a prime time for my pager to go off. It had been a long week of working outside in cold weather, and I was ready to have a quiet night at home.

I returned the call and the voice on the other end was high-pitched and shaking as a woman described the situation. Her Pit Bull had tangled with her Miniature Pinscher, and there was so much blood on both dogs, she wasn't sure who was more badly injured.

"Have you separated the dogs?" I asked.

"Yes, and Maximus is sneezing and shaking his head and spraying blood everywhere!"

"Where is the little dog right now?"

"Oh, Maximus is the little dog. Bailey, the Pit Bull is under the bed. He's afraid of Maximus!"

I asked a few more questions and concluded that Maximus had a bloody nose.

"Now Bailey is over at his bowl eating. That's good, right?"

It was interesting that she seemed more concerned about the larger dog. Big dog, little dog altercations usually did not end well for the smaller dog, and I had seen broken necks, ruptured eyes, crushed chests. My mind raced with horrible possibilities and I offered to see the dogs right away.

After-hours fees can be steep. She suggested that we could avoid those fees by her bringing the dogs to my house, but after some cost discussion, we decided that a morning visit at the clinic would be just fine. She would monitor the dogs overnight and call if anything changed.

I cautioned her that the little dog was probably swallowing a lot of blood, and might vomit it back up later.

"I used to work for a vet, doctor. I know what to look for! Thanks so much, and we'll see you in the morning!"

At 10:30 p.m., the pager went off again. I returned the call, and this time she was hysterical.

"He's hemorrhaging from his stomach, Doctor!"

I explained again that swallowing a lot of blood could make the little dog vomit blood. As the after-hours costs had not changed since our last conversation, she decided again that they could wait until morning.

The pager was quiet for the remainder of the night, and at 8:30 a.m., there they were at the clinic, a woman in a motorcycle jacket with an eager Pit Bull Terrier on a leash. There was no sign of the Min Pin, and she assured me that he was here, just waiting in the car. Adrian, my vet technician, had already completed the paperwork and we ushered them into the exam room.

I checked Bailey over, noting some scrapes and dried blood splashes on his face. Everything else was normal. His short tail wagged happily throughout the exam, and he stood still while I opened his mouth, listened to his heart and lungs, and checked him over for injuries. Adrian gave him a biscuit and the owner asked if we could hold him while she went to the car to fetch the little guy.

We waited, glancing out the window occasionally. The phone rang twice, and a client came in to buy some cat food.

Finally I went out to the parking lot, where a rhinestone-encrusted backside struggled from a side door of a 1980-something Firebird. I peered in the car window to see her holding a noosed dog leash and trying to lasso a furious little black shape that careened around the interior of the car. Gleaming teeth appeared at my window as the shape noticed my presence.

I retreated to the clinic and dispatched Adrian to assist with the situation. Eventually she returned with the 11-pound dog struggling on the end of a clinic leash, snapping at everything within reach. The owner followed at a safe distance, then informed us that she had to get to work and would be back at lunchtime. She left with Bailey in tow.

We pulled Maximus into the exam room and I noted with interest his spiked collar and "Dogadeth" T-shirt. Adrian quickly had him muzzled and on the table, and I was able to complete my exam, finding the remnants of a bloody nose and some facial swelling and superficial scrapes, but no obvious fractures and no other injuries.

Listening to his lungs through the growling was impossible, but I reasoned that his pulmonary and respiratory function was probably adequate, given the acrobatic display in the car. Saliva bubbled from Maximus's clamped muzzle, but he was immobilized and helpless. I decided against trying to open his mouth.

The owner had declined X-rays, so Maximus received some anti-inflammatory pain medicine, some antibiotics and drugs to soothe his stomach, and was placed in a kennel until he could be picked up. He hunched furiously in a corner as the door was latched, spiked collar askew, and ignored the food and water bowls.

At lunch time, I was startled by a large biker in the waiting room wearing overalls. His beard was braided and tattoos covered both folded arms.

"I'm here to pick up Maximus!" he barked, obviously in a hurry.

Adrian nodded and headed for the back room. Scuffling sounds were audible, then a muffled shriek and the clanging of the cage door. She reappeared without Maximus, her finger in her mouth.

The big biker heaved a disgusted sigh, then marched to the back room, his bulk filling the door frame. Adrian hurried after him.

"Sir, please just let me just get him ..."

But the man was already at the cages. He opened the bottom cage and reached a cautious hand toward Maximus, who bolted for freedom and lost his footing on the slick floor tiles. He ran in place briefly, then in a frenzy flew at the man's ankles, grabbing hold of his overalls and shaking his head violently.

A high feminine-sounding shriek filled the air, and the big man frantically danced on tiptoes, arms waving as the wrathful teeth gnashed around him. He collided with Adrian, knocking her to the floor. Still shrieking, he pranced in place as Adrian struggled to snare Maximus with the leash from her position on the floor. She scrambled to her feet and firmly parked the leash in the man's hands.

He retreated to the front door, still prancing on tiptoe and shrieking, leash at arm's length as Maximus struggled to sink his teeth into whatever he could grab and Adrian whisked the little dog into a spare pet carrier and handed it to the dancing biker. My explanations of the exam, medications, and follow-up care were largely unheard, and man and dog disappeared into an idling truck and sped away.

Later the owner called. Maximus was doing fine, she said. But there was just one thing.

"Doctor, my boyfriend was very upset today when he came home with Maximus. He said that your staff could use some extra training in dog handling!"

# Feral Cats

The cat carriers were stacked against the wall of the waiting room when I arrived at the clinic, and there was Maggie in her police uniform, happily reading yesterday's newspaper. She beamed when I entered, and waved an arm at the wall.

"I have a whole bunch of ferals today, doc! I don't know how many males or females, but some of them are friendly, so hopefully they won't give you too hard of a time!" And she finished her coffee, and headed out the door, paper under her arm.

I liked Maggie. She was tireless in her quest to see every last barn cat spayed or neutered, and we did quite a few for her. It was nice to have a new approach to stabilizing the wild cat population, as so many ranchers seemed to take a perverse pleasure in taking population control methods into their own hands. We'd notch the ear of every wild cat so there was no mistaking who was who, and the ranchers had been surprisingly cooperative, provided the bills didn't come their way. Fortunately, there was private funding for the project.

If the cat was truly feral, we wouldn't even attempt to handle it. The carrier would be flipped on its end, sliding the hissing occupant onto its backside against the door. A quick shot of a general anesthetic into the cat's muscle, a squall of rage from the cat, then peace as she or he slid into a drugged sleep. Even sedated the cats could be dangerous and it was prudent to be cautious. We'd wear heavy gloves until the cat was completely anesthetized.

While many of the cats were fairly healthy, most had intestinal worms and several had worse problems like masses in the abdomen, skin infections, dental problems, and a few were carriers of feline leukemia, a contagious virus usually fatal to cats. If the medical problem was untreatable, we would euthanize the suffering cat.

Adrian always enjoyed the cat work, and her handling skills were remarkable. She could coax the most fearful animal to her arms and restrain the most aggressive of cats for a blood draw. But even Adrian was wary of the ferals.

"Doc, you have to respect an animal that can bite into your joints!"

I agreed. There was something about a feral cat that was humbling, and something fearsome about the look in their eyes. I'd take a mean horse any day of the week over a mean cat.

Little Pandora, however, didn't seem like one that we needed to worry about. She was a chubby little calico, almost hyperactive in her affectionate overtures through the grid of the carrier door. She treaded, purred, reached arched paws through the door, and drove her face against your hand with a thud.

Adrian felt confident that we could restrain her for a blood draw and to clip her belly to check for a spay scar. We took her gently from her carrier, moved into the exam room and closed the door.

The exam room had a big window that looked out into the front waiting room, and I saw a woman standing outside the clinic front door talking on her cell phone. We were able to successfully draw blood on Pandora, and Adrian expertly flipped her onto her back so I could shave her belly to check for a spay scar.

I had just picked up the clippers when I heard the front door jingle, and the client walked in, phone in hand. Adrian and I were the only two in the clinic that day, and since she had the cat in her hands, I went out to help the lady.

She was clutching her phone, and tears filled her eyes. Through the exam room window, I could see Adrian, patiently stroking the cat. The woman burst into sobs and in heavily accented English stammered that she was afraid that her dog had cancer. It was hard to understand her, and I took my time asking questions, nodding reassuringly and patting her on the arm. Adrian gestured at me once and I shook my head at her.

The crying woman went on and on, and the clock in the waiting room ticked off the minutes. Adrian was starting to make faces at me through the window, and I made apologetic grimaces when the client wasn't looking, trying not to think of the wall of cats waiting for us.

The woman started a new line of questions, and suddenly, over her shoulder, I saw a calico object leap over Adrian's head. Adrian disappeared briefly. Then cat and Adrian sailed past the window and went out of sight again. Hind legs appeared, then Adrian's arm, then both crashed against the door. The woman turned slightly at the crash, but went on with her tale, and I struggled to maintain my sympathetic expression.

Now Adrian's head and upper body bobbed in a circle, and I could tell that she was chasing the cat around the exam table. A dreadful wailing emerged from the exam room, and the cat launched into the air again and Adrian followed. Biting the inside of my cheek hard, I focused desperately on the conversation at hand. Only the imagined consequences of losing my composure enabled me to keep a straight face, and finally, finally, the woman ended her tearful interrogation and left.

I collapsed onto the waiting room bench and laughed until I cried, Adrian glaring at me through the now foggy window. The cat was completely out of sight.

The exam room was a disaster, cat hair everywhere, a stethoscope on the floor, paper towels unrolled. Adrian was livid and her black expression deepened each time I bit back a smile or choked a laugh into a cough. The disheveled cat was drooling and panting, flattened on the table by Adrian's iron hands. And when we finally clipped her abdomen, of course she was already spayed, a neat tattoo outlining the spay scar.

Adrian spoke little for the rest of the day, grinning widely once when a quick paw slashed a bloody track down my arm. We worked through the rest of the cats in semi-silence, and at the end of the day, she marched home, jaw squarely set.

For weeks afterward, I'd catch myself snickering, and even today, when I am talking to a client in the waiting room, I have to look away from the exam room window.

# A Litter of Kittens

The feral cat spay and neuter program had been going very well, and the ranchers were starting to bring the cats in directly, rather than waiting for animal control to come out and set the humane traps. We supplied the traps and the wet cat food to use as bait, and they did the rest.

It was becoming a contest to some to see how many cats the men could trap and stack in the beds of the ranch trucks. One morning, two cat-laden pickups drag raced up the road, each trying to make it into the clinic driveway first. Shortly after, a police cruiser pulled in with flashing lights and the contrite ranchers stood in a huddle with the officer for twenty minutes, blocking our parking lot entrance.

Most of the ranchers were good about collecting the cats after the surgeries were completed, but there were a few who "forgot" to return for them, so we initiated the county's first cat-delivery system. Adrian joked that we should use an old ice cream truck for the deliveries, and play pre-recorded meowing over the speakers. I figured relations were shaky enough with the ranchers without adding that in, but it was an entertaining mental image nonetheless.

We were nearing the end of another long day of spaying and neutering feral cats when the front door jingled. Adrian stuck her head out to see a teen-age boy holding a cardboard box in his arms. She let him know that we'd be out as soon as we could, and if he'd just take a seat in the meantime, there were some magazines on the table. There was a period of silence, then the door jingled again.

"Hello?" Adrian called.

No response. Adrian walked into the waiting room to find the cardboard box resting on the bench. The room was otherwise empty.

I was closing up a spay incision and didn't look up as she returned.

"Uh, are you almost finished? Because you really have to see this!" she said in a strange voice.

I nodded toward the anesthesia machine and she clicked it off. I finished tying my knot, buried it, and snapped off my gloves. She took over monitoring the patient, and I headed to the exam room.

The box sat on the exam table and I peered into it and couldn't make immediate sense of what I was seeing. A foul odor rose from the interior and noisy mewing sounds echoed around the walls of the box. It was a nest of newborn kittens, but they were squirming in place, anchored together by something. I lifted the soiled towel that they rested on and brought them in a stinking, complaining tangle out of the box.

I had never seen anything like this in my career. The tiny creatures, eyes still tightly closed, were attached to a semisolid mass of necrotic tissue by the umbilical cords still attached to their bellies! Six of them were living and a seventh dead one dangled off to the side.

Adrian returned, having safely stowed the spay in a recovery cage, and after a quick huddle we got to work. She adjusted the lights expertly, and I gloved up and laid out some clamps and suture. One by one, we clamped each tiny umbilical cord, tied it off and freed each squirming kitten. Each got a gentle bath and massage with a warm rag and went into a clean box.

Five of the kittens were surprisingly vigorous, the sixth

lethargic and not moving much. We disposed of the stinking remains as quickly as possible, hauling it to the outside dumpster in back. Even with the clinic windows opened wide, the smell lingered, and Adrian sprayed some citrus odor remover around the room.

As near as I could figure, the mother cat simply had not cleaned up as each kitten was born. At the end, she had vanished for unknown reasons, leaving the newborns immobilized on their own placentas. It was hard to say how long they had been like that, but by the smell, it had to have been quite a while. I didn't see how they could have survived without nursing, but without a human to question, we were guessing.

I was prepared to tube feed but each kitten took a small bottle well, even the lethargic one, and they went into a cage with a warm-water heating pad, well-wrapped in towels. We didn't offer them too much formula initially, but fed small amounts every two hours until they were taking the full amount easily. Their vitals remained stable, their bowels and bladder worked normally, and they ate and slept in a normal newborn pattern.

We had a few foster homes that we relied on, and got the litter settled into a nearby location once we felt that they were ready to be moved. The six little creatures thrived on the formula and the good care, and grew quickly. Eventually their eyes opened, and they tussled and rolled on shaky legs, their tails fuzzy exclamation points. When they were old enough, they were spayed and neutered, and each one found a good home.

Adrian's comment that this was one for the books was prophetic. I have never seen anything like it before or since. The foster family ended up adopting two of the kittens, naming them "Half Hitch" and "Twister," and they are enormous, good-natured cats whom I see regularly.

# Horse Vibrations

Animal communicators deserve their own chapter. Every vet, large or small, has probably felt the pain as the client gushes about recently revealed revelations regarding Fluffy's feelings and requests a prescription medication or some expensive diagnostic that the communicator claimed the animal needed.

There may be vets out there who actively work with these communicators, but I am not one of them. I have enough trouble retaining credibility with my clients without deferring to a large, middle-aged woman with eagle feathers in her hair and turquoise jewelry rattling in sync with her spiritual vibrations as she diagnoses my patient for me.

It's even worse when the wide-eyed client, usually several-hundred dollars poorer, tells you that there was no way the communicator could have known these certain things that they revealed about the dog/cat/horse/gerbil. Usually they're right about that. The communicator didn't have any way of knowing these certain things that they revealed. The funny thing about these gems of insight is that they are usually things that the client has no way of knowing either, and there is no possible way to validate the claims. They usually include the dream that Fluffy had last night, the secret desires he has to own that shiny new collar/saddle, and the trauma he suffered as a puppy/kitten/foal/guppy.

These people do have one real gift. They're often very insightful and very talented at getting their facts directly from the source, which happens to be the owner. They'll engage the owner in deep conversation, then later in the reading will use something the client inadvertently revealed and won't remember saying.

I believe in non-verbal communication, and I know that animals can communicate certain things to humans and to each other. But I do not believe the tripe concocted by most animal communicators, particularly when they are taking people's money.

Early in my career I thought I could expose these people and simultaneously educate the client, so I would painstakingly work up whatever the communicator had "seen" when they read the animal's thoughts. I radiographed skulls for hidden sinus masses and "headaches," ran lab tests on blood and urine and palpated abdomens for "liver and kidney pain," checked the heart for "occasional skipped beats and fatigue," and when I could not validate clinically the observations of the psychics, I'd wait happily for the owner to denounce the communicator. Yet the fault was almost always mine for failing to confirm the psychic visions.

I didn't retain a lot of these people as long-term clients.

My most noteworthy animal communicator story centers around a horse named Ironman. It is not a happy story. Ironman was a large black Trakehner show-jumper that had been severely abused in several show barns and had cracked up mentally. He had nearly killed a groom for trying to take off his blanket when he was eating, and had been "rescued" by a well-intended but seriously misguided woman.

When his new owner, a tiny red-headed woman with dark circles under her eyes, started working with him and riding him, he'd periodically grab her with his teeth and shake her like a dog shakes its prey. Once, he seized a friend of mine by the clothing (and skin) around her waist and lifted her into the air, and it took three barn workers with pitchforks to get him to drop her. She had awful bruises on her abdomen.

The problem was that Ironman was a beautiful jumper and won everything he competed in. Riders joked that the judges were too scared of him not to award him first place. The ribbons apparently outweighed the "minor safety issues," according to the owner, and it was just that no one understood Ironman properly. If he lunged at the owner, or injured her, he was "having a bad day" and she should have recognized it and helped him through it rather than stressing him out further.

To drive the point home, an animal communicator was brought in, and after Ironman ran her out of his stall, she decided she could do her communicating from the barn aisle. As he lunged at her through the bars on his stall door, she explained in a misty voice that the owner and Ironman had been lovers in a past life and that the owner had betrayed him, and now they were reunited to work through their trust issues so they could both move forward in life.

To soothe Ironman, pictures of him as a foal were hung where he could see them and reflect on happier times, and herbal bundles were tucked behind the pictures. Crystals to balance him were also hung around the stall. The guilty owner was given specific instructions on how to redeem herself to her horse. She was relieved to finally understand his issues, and was anxious to begin the healing.

Ironman was terrifying in his unpredictability. On several occasions I had performed dental work on him. Strangely, he didn't mind shots, but I always gave him extra drugs to sedate him, as I would have to have my hands in his mouth. You couldn't enter his stall abruptly or he would attack you. If you could coax him into sticking his head out into the aisle, he was more or less OK when the lead rope was snapped onto his halter, but he'd still occasionally take a chunk out of his handler.

He shared a paddock with an older, quiet gelding that was also a patient of mine, and I would occasionally need to enter the fenced space to look at something on the older horse. All Ironman had to do was lift his head suddenly and lock me into his sights, his head pointed at me like an arrow, and I was over the fence like an Olympian. I wasn't taking any chances.

Most of the barn workers bore wounds on their person from the wrath of the jilted Ironman, and why the barn didn't evict him was a mystery to me. There were signs all over his stall door, in English and Spanish, warning away the unwary. Interestingly, the Spanish sign that was supposed to read "Caution, this horse may bite," translated into, "Caution, this horse is purple."

The Spanish-speaking barn employees laughed for weeks. If Ironman was working in the arena, they'd point and warn each other about the dangerous "purple" horse.

But no one was laughing when Ironman attacked an unsuspecting young man who was cleaning his stall and sent him to the hospital with a fractured arm and a concussion. Enough was enough. Ironman and his owner were evicted, and several people, including me, told the owner to put the horse down before he killed someone.

I received a call a few weeks later from a friend. Ironman was installed in a facility an hour away that I worked for occasionally. We had a long talk, and she assured me that the staff had been properly warned and they could handle him. A lot of Ironman's former barn workers had family at the new place, and I figured that the stories about Ironman would have already been passed on, and that everyone would stay safe.

I was wrong.

The third day after Ironman's arrival at the new barn, he attacked a valuable horse in an adjoining stall. The horse survived, but was badly injured. The barn owner and workers again had to go after Ironman with pitchforks to get him off the other horse, who was swiftly transported to a hospital for surgery. During the tussle, Ironman's blanket had been torn and was twisted on his torso.

The woman who was managing the barn came in late that day

and was unaware of the situation with the other horse. Clearly she hadn't gotten the memo about Ironman's mental state. She saw the twisted blanket and quickly entered Ironman's stall to take it off of him. He gave no warning and the attack was swift and silent. He grabbed her by the face and threw her against the wall, then went after her with his front feet. She was able to crawl away from him, holding her cheek, which had been torn from her jaw, in place with one hand.

The barn owner was a few stalls down from Ironman's and heard nothing except a thud and a quiet moan. She looked out into the aisle to see the injured manager at the sink frantically rinsing her face, a trail of blood across the floor. Realizing what had happened, she called her husband, who arrived at the barn with a gun, ready to shoot the horse. Ironman was spared the gun due to the tearful pleas of the hysterical owner who by now had arrived.

The barn manager was taken to the hospital, where a plastic surgeon had to piece her face back together. She was relatively calm about the situation and at that time didn't want to involve the police, despite advice to the contrary.

A week passed, and I had not heard anything new about the situation. Then my phone rang – a client who operated a children's riding camp wanted me to do a vet check on a new horse, a black Trakehner named Ironman that had been donated to the program. I quickly told her everything I knew. My next call was to the police.

The owner was served with papers detailing that she was harboring a dangerous animal and would be fully liable if he injured anyone else. She accepted and signed the papers and started making plans to build a safe enclosure for Ironman with a high electric wire running around it. Fortunately her husband had had enough and ordered Ironman euthanized. Within a week it was done.

Ironman got an expensive marker on his grave. The barn manager got long scars running from the corner of her mouth across her cheek and tooth mark shaped scars under her eye, which she'll carry for the rest of her life. Ironman's owner got a new horse. He had been abused in a show barn and could be a little unpredictable, and the animal communicator felt that he had been orphaned as a foal and had an attachment disorder. The new horse got herb bundles and crystals hung in his stall and baby pictures hung where he could see them. It wasn't clear if he and the owner had been lovers in a past life.

# Clients from Hell

*Horse owner: "Why is my horse wearing this blanket?"*

*Barn Worker: "You said to blanket him if it was below 32F!"*

*Horse Owner: "No! I said to blanket him with the BLUE blanket if it was below 32F. This blanket isn't blue, is it? Well, IS IT? What color is this blanket?!"*

*Barn Worker: "Um, grayish blue?"*

*Horse Owner: "It's called teal. TEAL! Teal is not blue! The blue blanket is in his tack trunk on the other side of the barn! Oh, I'll just get it MYSELF!" [She stomps away]*

*Barn Worker: "And that woman has children? God help them."*

*Me: "Yes, but only two remaining. She ate the others."*

# Clients from Hell: Act 1

*Client: "Dr Diehl, I am so sorry to keep you waiting!"*

*Me: "No, you're fine—I'm just glad I have the right place! I thought I saw you near the barn but then you disappeared!"*

*Client: "Um. I'm a little embarrassed."*

*Me: "Is everything ok?"*

*Client: "Well, it's just that...I sort of thought you were a bear!"*

*Me: "With a blue hat on?"*

*Client: "Well, I didn't see the hat. I just saw the big brown coat you had on, and it was just the way you were staggering up my driveway. You looked like a bear!"*

*Me: "Yes, the driveway was pretty icy. I couldn't make the last 1/8th of a mile, so I had to leave the truck at the bottom of the hill."*

*Client: "Maybe you could wear an orange hat next time."*

*Me: "Or you could sand the driveway. Most bears can't drive."...*

When you're a horse vet, you meet and work with some wonderful people. You'll be exposed to a wide variety of breeds, disciplines, and personality types. It is rewarding and fun, and great clients make it all worth it. But there are a few types that you need to identify and steer clear of. They'll drain your sanity, your serenity and kick holes in your self-confidence if you let them. I'll introduce them one by one in the next few pages.

When you're a horse vet, your credibility is tested constantly. Maybe you look too young, look too pretty, maybe you're too nice or not nice enough. Maybe a woman shouldn't be doing a "man's job." Maybe the moon was wrong that day. Who can say why one client loves you and another can't stand you. There will be a percentage of clients who appreciate you and will remain loyal to you, who make a hard day worth it. They celebrate your successes, understand when a case doesn't go well, and send good people your way.

Then there's the other kind. The clients who drop you with no explanation and you don't realize that you were fired until you see another vet working on what used to be your patient. If you come face to face with this client, they'll greet you with a "deer in the headlights" look. They'll talk a mile a minute and be fake friendly, but they won't mention the new vet on board and neither will you.

You'll also come up against former clients who drop you with no explanation and then malign you to anyone who will listen for offenses that you probably didn't commit. These people ignore you when you are in the barn, and you'll receive no feedback from them that could help you do better next time. If you enter a room while they're in it, any conversation taking place stops immediately and resumes as soon as you leave.

Let's not leave out the horse owner who will never call you even though they know nothing about you, yet they tell people that you aren't good with whatever procedure is popular that week because they've assigned expertise to another veterinarian who probably doesn't deserve the distinction any more than you deserve the snub.

Finally, we have the established client who calls in a "specialist" to "work with you" because you don't have the ability to figure out why "Misty Rainbow Chakra" turns her head away when the owner tries to bridle her, tosses her head and has reared several times under saddle. Perhaps you were even silly enough to suggest riding her with a longer rein and changing the bit to something less severe.

Enter the trainer who is certified in Reiki and crystal waving, the acupuncturist, the Natural homeopathy practitioner, Natural essential oils mixer, the saddle fitter, the animal communicator, the horse owner two stalls down, the Natural shoer, the equine lay-dentist who will equilibrate the mouth and adjust the skull for maximum performance, and the small animal vet who lives in Texas but has an opinion, and is really far away, so must be an expert.

You name it, they'll call them in, and you'll be relegated to two clicks above drooling idiot because you didn't cleanse the negative energy with crystals, perform equilibration of the mouth, adjust the skull, pour green glop down their throat, carve the feet into square barefoot blocks and sell them a three-hundred dollar magnetized saddle pad. It's especially painful when you're allowed to remain in the loop, but your phone rings constantly with your new "team" of caregivers handing you their assessment and recommendations for what you thought was your patient, the client demanding your compliance and cooperation.

There's a whole spectrum of toxic clients out there. But to simplify things a little, I've created a few categories in which most can be grouped. I share these stories in the hopes that other unsuspecting equine vets will recognize the warning signs and flee quickly before engaging.

In category number one, we have Phoebe Pills, a client to

actively avoid. In my career, I have met several Phoebes, and have been equally caught off guard each time by their tactics. To engage with a Phoebe is to enter a setup for utter and complete failure. You'll notice that God also makes it into Phoebe's story. This was another one that I could not handle on my own.

Interestingly I had done work for this particular Phoebe before the trouble started, and everything had gone fine. Perhaps her personal life had changed, or her financial situation had become dire. Either way I had no idea what I was driving into when I pulled up to her farm at lunchtime. I was there to do some dental work on a few horses.

When Jillian and I arrived, Phoebe Pills, who was wearing filthy clothes and had a disheveled braid draped over her shoulder, greeted us in the driveway with a forlorn looking cat, ear drooping to the side. At her request, I knelt down and examined the animal, and discovered a rather bloody mass of tissue occluding the ear canal. When I nudged it with a finger, the cat moaned and huddled to the ground.

This was unscheduled, but these types of things were a common occurrence in my day. The mass would have to come off and I'd have to make time in my packed schedule to deal with it.

I infiltrated the mass with a local anesthetic, waited until it was numb, then snipped it off with a pair of Metzenbaum scissors, holding pressure on the ear to stop the bleeding. The cat was not cooperative, and we finally wrapped it in a towel. I dispensed some antibiotics and some drops for the ear, and suggested we send the mass off to the lab for analysis. This was declined, so Jillian and I cleaned up, and laid out our instruments for the horse dentals.

I looked at the clock. We were 45 minutes behind schedule already. I did all of the dental work that she'd requested, then fielded veterinary questions from Phoebe for another 30 minutes about several other animals on the property. Everywhere I looked there was another creature, a cow in a filthy enclosure, two gigantic mules in a weedy field, a litter of piglets in a muddy pen. I also refilled some expensive prescription medicine for another patient, and changed a bandage on a goat's leg.

As we were packing up, Phoebe dragged over a crippled llama for me to look at, taking up another 30 minutes of my time. Jillian had calculated the bill, including all of the add-on work, and presented it to Phoebe, who barely glanced at it. Jillian explained all of the charges and gave Phoebe the total amount due.

Phoebe didn't dispute the presented total. But, "You'll have to bill me. I think my husband took the checkbook," she said, without looking for her checkbook.

Jillian looked at me, and naively I nodded. I had worked for Phoebe before and she had paid me, so I assumed I was OK to bill her.

We emailed her the invoice that evening, and I know she got it, as she replied to the email. For good measure I mailed her a bill as well. No payment showed up in the mail, and after 25 days, I sent her another bill.

A week later, a crumpled envelope showed up in the mail with Phoebe's name on the return address. A torn check for less than half of the cost of the horse dentals was made out in a furious scrawl to a misspelled version of my personal name, omitting the "Dr." or "DVM." In the memo line, a sarcastic question mark had been scribbled so viciously that the pen had gone through the paper.

A letter to me in the same furious scrawl was enclosed, and the exclamation points berated me as I read the outraged words. "Are you serious!!! How dare you ...!!! ...Overcharged what you quoted me ...!!! ...I rescued all of these animals that you worked on!!! ...You have no compassion!!! ... Greedy!!... Ridiculous to charge for the llama ...!!!" and on and on.

Thinking stupidly that this could be sorted out, I had Jillian call her to go over the charges again and to remind her that at her request, we had done far more vet work than just the dentals, never mind all of the drugs she'd gotten from us. Jillian called the next day to tell me that she had never been screamed at in such a way by anyone, and that the woman had lost her voice several times, she was screaming so hard. The small check cleared, so I decided to let matters lie, and simply mail another bill.

Then the emails started and the hang-up phone calls. The emails attacked me on every level from professional to ethical, accused me of all sorts of dreadful behaviors, told me what a horrible vet I was, and were all rambling and irrational with erratic spelling and punctuation. I reached a point where I stopped reading them through, just saved them in a folder with Phoebe's name on it. If I responded, my emails were always bland and cordial, but spelled out the consequences of sending her to collections if she failed to pay her bill in full.

I dreaded checking my emails, for fear that another hate missive bearing her name would pop up. I dreaded sending her bills, as another flood of furious and vicious emails would result. The situation dragged on. The hang-up phone calls intensified. I was always looking over my shoulder for her when I was in town, fearing a public confrontation.

I did see her once at a horse auction, and she was in a huddle with some women I didn't know. All were sending unfriendly looks my way. I walked past them once, and overheard my name from the hissed conversation they were having. Part of me wanted to march over and let Phoebe have it. Fortunately, I had the sense to say a quick prayer and was able to keep my temper in check. I just walked by and smiled.

Then Phoebe really went on the warpath with her emails and hang-up calls. If I thought I'd been getting a verbal beating before, I realized that she'd only been warming up. Apparently seeing me up close had renewed her wrath. I tried not to read the hate missives, but it was hard to miss the opening lines that burned into my brain and some days would play on repeat.

Finally, in a rare personal response, I wrote to her that I was sorry that she was having a hard time and hoped her personal life would improve. I wrote that I would pray for her, while secretly having no actual intention of doing so. She responded sarcastically, "Yes. Me too."

One of the most dishonest things that I could do would be to claim to be praying for someone when I wasn't. It was just that level of hypocrisy that I hated, and I realized that I had committed myself with my words. I had left myself no choice but to do what I said I would.

So I prayed for Phoebe through gritted teeth. I didn't want to, and it was a huge effort for a while. At first, the best I could do was to pray for an abundance of God's will in her life. What I really wanted was for God to skewer her with a lightning bolt. But I kept at it. Eventually I was able to pray for peace to come into her life. I prayed for her to receive love and kindness. And I prayed for myself to remain honest, focus on my own behavior and change what I could, and remember that the only thing that separated me from Phoebe was, well, not a whole lot. It kept me sane during this challenging time.

I won't say the prayers changed Phoebe's behavior one iota, but they definitely changed mine over the next six months. I no longer laid awake at night rehashing the incident and how unfair it all was. Phoebe's face no longer appeared before me at odd times, leaving me gnashing my teeth and muttering furiously. I no longer felt anger or the desire to punish her, and I was able to forgive her behavior, while continuing to pursue fair payment for my services. I let the whole thing go, just kept on her with the bills, and after firing off a few more email potshots at me, she paid the balance in full. I have heard nothing more from her.

# Clients from Hell: Act 2

Next up on the client-from-hell-list is Vendetta Mooch, who usually is your first caller when you start up your new practice. Vendetta owns, well, a lot of horses. Even she's not sure how many she has. But they're not really all hers. One belongs to her niece, two to her friend's daughter, several more to some friends in other states, and so on. She'll inform you proudly that several more are "rescues." You'll notice that there seem to be quite a few visibly pregnant mares in the herd and Vendetta will assure you that those were accidental breedings.

The Vendettas are usually in their mid-fifties, and the husbands aren't around much, but there are usually two or three rough-looking females hanging around who treat Vendetta with hero worship. They speak in raspy cigarette voices, and look at you suspiciously when you speak. Vendetta usually wears ratty jeans, sneakers, and a hoodie sweatshirt. She's overweight, doesn't spend a lot of time combing her hair or cleaning her house, and says things like "I seen" and "stove up," as in, "the horse isn't feeling well, he's all stove up."

Vendetta will court you and make you feel like you just might be the finest veterinarian on this side of the continent, even though you have yet to actually do any vet work for her. What you don't yet know is that Vendetta has gone through every vet in town and owes most of them money.

You'll spend a lot of time on the phone with Vendetta before you actually go out to her place, and she'll extract a lot of free veterinary advice from you in the guise of flattery. You just assume you're building a relationship with a great new client, so you don't hesitate to hand it out. Vendetta will also tell you story after story about idiot vets, and vet stupidity, and cast herself in the victim role. You won't be like those idiot vets, you will assure her! You are smarter and better than that, and you're delighted that here's a client who can really see your inner talent!

Vendetta decides she'll do you the favor of having you come out and geld some colts. She's careful to lock you into a price without bothering to tell you that all of the colts are huge, wild and there's really no good place to work on them. She'll also have a lot of additional work that she doesn't mention on the phone and figures will get left off the bill.

So, confidently, you show up on the scheduled day and time, and after four filth-splattered hours, large bruises on your shin and thigh, torn clothing, and only two of the three colts gelded, and a lot of time talking and answering questions about numerous other animals, you give up and hand her a bill. Because your quoted cost didn't allow for extra time, extra drugs, or personal injury, you feel like you can't charge Vendetta more. You also had to cancel your last appointment of the day because you were running so late.

So now you've lost money, lost another call, have to buy new pants, and Vendetta decides she can't pay the full amount today, and you'll have to bill her. You might see the rest of it several months later, but she'll ignore any late charges you might think to add, and those charges will sit in the balance column of overdue accounts as a reminder to you to not ever work for Vendetta again. And congratulations, you're now the new star of Vendetta's idiot vet tales!

# Clients from Hell: Act 3

You can't practice in large barns without encountering Jessamine. Jessamine is always, always wearing riding clothes and her face is lined and hard, with weasel eyes. If she smiles, it doesn't change the hardness of her gaze one bit, and is, in fact, terrifying. If you see her at the supermarket, she's wearing riding clothes. If you bump into her in a restaurant, she's wearing riding clothes. She probably sleeps in them. And she never takes off her riding gloves either, but as her hands are usually clenched into tight fists, you may not notice them right away.

Jessamine usually is at the barn, browbeating her riders in a corner of the arena or fighting with a lathered horse with rolling eyes. Her training credentials are a bit of a mystery, but there's probably a weekend Parelli clinic or two in there somewhere, as well as several internet certifications. If she's on a horse, you can spot her immediately by her laser straight reins, her bulging biceps and rigid body that jounces unpleasantly in the saddle, the horse's movements pulled into a labored rocking-horse gait and mouth drawn wide open against the bit.

You'll also see her putting horses and unprepared riders over terrifyingly oversized jumps, or maybe you'll just hear the crashing of feet knocking poles to the ground and the chaotic sounds of unbalanced horses and riders trying to land their erratic flight patterns. If one of her students hasn't already broken a collarbone, they will soon. And if you look closely at the stumbling horse, it is likely to be the one that you and the farrier recommended not be jumped ever again.

Aside from being an expert rider and expert trainer, Jessamine feels that she is practically a vet, as well as an expert judge of horseshoers. After all, she worked in a clinic as an assistant ten years ago. She'll tell you anything you might want to know about any horse disease and how she feels it needs to be treated. She likes to incorrectly diagnose her rider's horses with the trendy disease of the season, usually gleaned from the pages of whatever horse magazine she's currently reading, and heaven help you if you fail to validate her medical findings. If you checked her tack trunk, you'd find numerous bottles of injectable drugs and syringes, and she often parades around the barn with her stethoscope draped firmly around her neck.

She name-drops famous vets and lets you know immediately that she is "dear friends" with so and so, and will be consulting with them on any case you'll be unlucky enough to tend to under Jessamine's gimlet eye. Or without telling anyone, she may simply load your patient into her own trailer and march them down to the "expert" on her own. You won't hear another thing about this case, nor will you ever be asked to treat it again.

Jessamine will never call you directly, but one of her riders might, although Jessamine will try her hardest to steer them away from you and toward whichever vet she feels will do what she wants. She also is sure that she's an expert judge of farriers, and will malign the work of the most seasoned certified journeyman farrier in favor of her inept favorite of the month, whom she'll try to force on anyone who rides with her.

The only comfort here is the high level of predictability in your interactions with Jessamine. Whatever your diagnosis, Jessamine will disagree – never to you directly, but to your client. If she's polite to you, you know that she's got an ulterior motive lurking behind the Noh mask of friendliness. When you leave Jessamine's company, you can be certain that when you're out of earshot, she'll be loudly dissecting your many examples of veterinary incompetence to whomever she can corner.

There won't be many surprises in your dealings with her, so just weather her presence and take comfort in knowing that since she hates everyone, most notably herself, none of the bad behavior is personal and it becomes boring and even a little sad after a while. Maybe you'll even find the grace to forgive her and wish her a happier life from a safe distance. Maybe you'll even think to pray for her without making snarky comments about how God has his work cut out for him with this woman.

Overall it's a sad situation. You won't have a positive interaction with Jessamine. There will be several that you thought went well, but they didn't. Trust me.

# Clients from Hell: Act 4

In the final act, you'll meet a precious little female named Prima, whose world you've now entered. She's the last but the most deadly of them all, as she is really a witch disguised as a pert little princess. Prima has a darling little ponytail, always wears her imported riding britches that do not look like anyone else's riding britches, has her very own barn, a non-horsey husband who foots the bills and her own court of horse ladies who hang on her every word. Yes, you really did just see Prima whisper into one of her lady-in-waiting's ears, who giggled, then whispered something back.

Prima is the queen bee of queen bees. It's still high school in Prima's barn, 30 or so years later, and everybody stays obediently within their social strata. When Prima's lumpy ladies in expensive britches address her, their feet are together neatly, and they lean forward slightly in supplication, overwhelmed to be in her presence. Usually the ladies are considerably older than Prima, were unpopular in high school, and have just bought their very first horse, usually lame, and usually selected by Prima or one of her horse connections who probably took home a nice commission on the inside deal.

Whatever you do, do not mention the fact that the horse is lame, should you be unfortunate enough to have to vet it at some point. If you're there to float teeth or draw blood or vaccinate, do those things, get paid, then leave. If they want to know why their horse isn't "collecting," "picking up the right lead," or while not lame "is just off," don't just walk away – run. Sorry, but there's a horse colicking down the road and you have to leave immediately!

If you are silly enough to comment on the lameness, the owner and Prima will either be mortally offended that you called this amazing animal lame, or that you couldn't glance at the horse, diagnose the problem and fix it within 20 minutes with any of the following therapies: Reiki, acupressure, chiropractic, acupuncture, homeopathy, supplements or animal communication.

It's very simple: If you didn't see it, you don't have to go there. Save the lameness exams for the owners who are mentally stable enough to deal with them.

When you and Prima have your very first conversation, she'll hand you her business card with a picture of Prima and a very fancy horse performing a contrived looking extended trot. This way, you'll know exactly who you're talking to. In the picture, Prima is immaculately clad in proper dressage attire, her hair netted decorously into a low bun, and the list of initials and accolades below her name would baffle the most sophisticated CIA code breaker.

If you actually research Prima's list of accolades and accomplishments, you'll learn that while she did struggle up through the ranks of whatever organization she claims to be affiliated with, her performance was marginal at best. You'll learn that CURCHA stands for "Certified in Usui Reiki Crystal Healing and Aromatherapy." You'll learn that respectable trainers labor for weeks to undo the damage that Prima's riding instruction has caused to the students who get wise and switch barns. You'll also learn that Prima's non-horsey husband has no idea that she's having an affair with a Natural Horsemanship trainer.

For Prima is a certified Natural horse enthusiast. Her

horseshoer is a certified Natural shoer whom she tries to force on anyone who rides with her and her horses get Natural acupuncture and Natural homeopathy and the stalls have to be sprayed with Natural Tea Tree Oil because everything has to be Natural in her barn. There's also a surround-sound system in Prima's barn so you can enjoy Yanni moaning from every corner.

Crystals hang from every window, and Natural Supplements from a pyramid marketing scheme that she tries to sell everyone are stacked in her office. You'll find powders to stimulate the immune system, detoxify the liver, build bone strength, prevent colic, promote vision, cure arthritis. Every brainwashed boarder has bought enough of Prima's Natural Supplements to advance Prima to Master Natural Supplement Seller status. The certification hangs on the office wall, and the "M.N.S.S." follows Prima's name on her business card.

Don't worry. You won't be Natural enough for Prima, or at least that's what she'll tell herself. The truth is when you question her Natural Healing abilities and she realizes that your IQ is almost double what hers is, you won't ever be asked back. And she'll see to it that none of her ladies or any of her little friends will ever call you either. Eventually you'll notice that she is the common denominator in most of your lost business.

# Forgive the Clients from Hell

Protect your sanity and your professional integrity. Do your best to quickly identify these challenging types so that they don't catch you unaware. Use their unavoidable presence in your life to gain valuable lessons, and also to appreciate your non-toxic, pleasant clients more! Most importantly, don't take them personally. You aren't the first to run afoul of them, and you will definitely not be the last. People like these will make you crazy if you let them.

Forgiveness is not an easy concept for those of us who feel that we have been treated unfairly by another person. Why should we forgive someone who we feel deserves punishment for what they have done to us? We want the world to know how wronged  we were, and in case the world doesn't know, we tell the story over and over, casting ourselves as the victim and portraying the other person in the worst light possible. We want the world to punish this person and we want to feel vindicated!

There are several large problems created by our need for justice when someone has treated us badly. Telling others the story of the hurtful situation keeps it alive and right in front of our field of vision, blocking out any positive things we might encounter during the day. Reliving it constantly makes it bigger than it really was. We tend to eliminate any details about our own actions, taking care to make the other person completely at fault. We nurse the resentment and sip from it throughout the day, poisoning ourselves through the waking hours. At night, we wake at odd hours and rehash the incident over and over.

To forgive does not mean to enable someone else and make their bad behavior OK. This is one of the most commonly used excuses for not forgiving another. To forgive is to recognize that another human being is spiritually sick, and that more than likely they do not know any better. It acknowledges our own powerlessness against the actions of others. It also puts us on a platform of empathy where we can relate to the other person's actions and be reminded of times when our own behavior wasn't perfect either.

To forgive is to release ourselves from the self-righteous and consuming need for vengeance. We give that to God – the one who is best equipped to deal with it. Forgiveness demonstrates faith. It is saying, God, I trust you. You've got this and you'll deal with it as you see fit, and I can let go. Forgiveness frees us from the desire to force another person to change, and keeps the focus where it belongs – on God and on our own behavior.

When we can recognize spiritual sickness in another, we can acknowledge that there were times in our own lives when we behaved similarly, and that we may do so again at some point. If we deserve forgiveness for our own bad behavior, then so do others. To forgive is to acknowledge our shared humanity, and our equal capacity for spiritual sickness. It is a great opportunity for us to take ownership of those behaviors. The only person we can control and change is ourselves.

There is a great quote from the poet Clarissa Pinkola Estes: "How does one know if she has forgiven? You tend to feel sorrow over the circumstance instead of rage; you tend to feel sorry for the person rather than angry with him. You tend to have nothing left to say about it all."

# The Snake in the Grass

When we settled on FriendlyTown, everything we had researched pointed to the conclusion that there was work for me and a place for me, and that I would not be hurting anyone's business. The vets that I spoke to were friendly and welcoming, and were glad that I was coming. There was one, a Dr. Mutilate, who never returned any of my calls, but I didn't worry about it too much. I went around and met everyone in person, hoping to be seen as a supportive colleague, and all seemed well.

Apparently, however, Dr. Mutilate didn't get the memo, nor was he OK with my presence in his town. From day one, he took offense at my existence and went out of his way to be as hateful as possible. I was trying to be a good colleague, but it wasn't easy. He ignored me completely if we happened to be at the same barn on the same day. Clients would repeat horrible things he'd said about me, and his staff at the front desk of his clinic was openly critical of me to clients in their office. My policy was to keep tight-lipped if a client repeated hurtful things to me and quickly change the subject, but it really hurt my feelings.

To make matters worse, I had an avalanche of requests for second opinions on cases of his. I learned to bring a colleague along on some of these calls to photograph and videotape the horses, as the patient inevitably would be staggering around on a hopeless injury that had been simmering for weeks or sometimes months. Several clients described how they had been told to turn the horse out to pasture for six months. It was impossible to provide a medical opinion on these cases without implying certain things should have been done differently, and relations between Mutilate and me plummeted.

The clients were strangely careful about discussing Mutilate, saying things like, "He's a really good friend of mine, but he just doesn't seem to care about my horse's health. Of course he's such a great vet that maybe he's just too busy." This last sentence was usually uttered loudly, the speaker looking around furtively, as though Mutilate might parachute suddenly from the sky.

I'd hear, "He's always in a hurry. He has no time to do a thorough exam." Or worse, "He gets mad when I ask him questions." From what I was seeing, the man had lost his desire to practice any sort of high-quality medicine and relied on his bullying personality to steamroll the client. The people who were calling me had stopped trusting him and seemed afraid of him.

There was a cross-section of the clientele, however, who were diehard members of the "Mutilate-Hung-the-Moon" club. They'd speak of him in reverent tones, telling me what a "leg man" or "performance vet" he was. Mostly they were women, lonely and in need of a commanding male presence, and they had a unique ability to fail to see his shortcomings.

The "club" believed every word that Mutilate uttered, and should I be unlucky enough to blunder into a situation where I was asked to treat something of theirs, I could count on one of two things happening. Once Mutilate learned of the brief mutiny, either a club member would call and sweetly request all of the records from me, and then disappear, never to be heard from again; or Mutilate himself would demand the records from me and take the case over without a thank you or any other communication. I could also count on him to disagree loudly with whatever it was I'd done or recommended and insult me as part of the bargain.

When eventually I learned to avoid Mutilate's club of women and say no to any requests involving their horses, my life got a little easier. But I still saw his poor medicine and his misguided treatments. Colleagues were sharing their own horror stories and told long, sad tales of lousy care and suffering animals. I couldn't escape the wake of Mutilate, and his personal attacks on me intensified. A particularly nasty phone call from him left me speechless and shaking. I realized that he was nothing more than a bully who used intimidation and scare tactics to get his way, but he still frightened me.

All of this was having the wrong effect on me. Hurt and angry by his treatment of me, I now had a personal vendetta against him. I decided that his mishaps were to my benefit and made me look like a pretty great vet. I could smile disdainfully when faced with one of his colossal wrecks, make pitying comments about him, and feel pretty special about my greatness. I began to be openly critical of him and his staff, and ridiculed people who still used him.

I became nastier and nastier about him as time passed. It was a self-perpetuating mindset. I'd talk about him endlessly to my friends, at home, to my family. Yet inside, I was feeling uglier and meaner, and I'd wake at night gnawing over all the wrongs he'd done to me and to his patients and how I wanted to punish him. I said dreadful things about him, and repeated every negative story I knew about him, wanting to do him harm. But it didn't feel good to be cruel. It felt awful.

I started to break through the ugly mindset by consciously asking God to release my resentment and my bitterness. I really wanted God to make Mutilate disappear, and praying for someone that I thought I hated was painful and initially unrewarding. But I kept at it, realizing that regardless of his behavior, I was being poisoned by the situation and did not want to be that person. The damage I was doing to myself was not worth it.

It took a lot of conscious prayer and asking God to release me from the resentment and the bitterness. Often I had to repeat myself multiple times a day. I'd pray, go do something else, then be right back at bitterness and resentment. It was very frustrating at times, but as I practiced, I began to realize that as soon as I asked God to take the negativity and show me a better way through, it would be provided. The brief moments of peace, fleeting as they sometimes were, cleared a space of sanity in my tormented mind. As I began to experience the release from the bitterness, I sought the peace more and more, and the spaces of sanity grew and multiplied until it seemed that they had overwhelmed the negativity.

I'd never known freedom from the yelling voices of misery, and it had never occurred to me that there was another way to live. This could only be the work of a higher power – a being who was doing for me what I could not do for myself.

I reached a point where I thought of Mutilate very little, or if I did so, it was with humility. There were several more negative interactions, but their power to ruin my day/week/month was kept in check by keeping God involved. He would sort it out. It was God's fight, not mine, and there were more important things for me to focus my energies on.

One day I received a phone call from a vet who had moved to the area without checking with any of the resident vets to see if there would be room for him. The area was oversaturated already, and his presence was going to make it harder for all of us who were struggling to make a living. He came with a brand new vet truck, brand new equipment and no children. He informed me that he would be doing mainly cattle work, but I knew better, having already seen descriptions of horse work on his website.

Suddenly, I was in Mutilate's shoes, a new vet moving into "my" territory, and I had a sudden rush of empathy. He'd watched some of his longtime clients turn away from him and had driven past their farms, probably seeing my truck in their driveway. How would I feel under the same circumstances? How was I going to treat this new vet?

We met for coffee and the new vet played his part well, avoiding discussion about horse work and stressing his interest in food animal medicine and small animal medicine. He pretended to care about me and my family, and we had a friendly visit.

Several days later, he met with my colleague, a small animal vet, who thought it was nice that this young vet had such an interest in horse medicine, and my cow vet friend wished him luck as he embarked on his small animal veterinary career.

Several weeks later, a vet colleague who had formerly practiced in the same region as this new vet called me, as he'd heard that I was "selling out and leaving." It didn't take a rocket scientist to connect the dots.

Signs and ads for the new vet appeared all over town. Then he launched several horse vaccination clinics, undercutting everyone's prices by up to 30%. I saw him everywhere, poised at the rodeos, prowling the horse shows, driving through the boarding stables. He carefully avoided me, going out the back door of a barn as I entered the front.

I pictured Mutilate every time I wanted to get hostile or speak negatively. I won't say that my thoughts were always pretty, but my public behavior was impeccable. Nobody was going to witness me behaving unprofessionally or being a poor colleague.

I was so concerned about how this vet was affecting my business that I forgot completely about the other vets in town whose toes he was also stomping on. Apparently Mutilate, infuriated by the new vet's actions, decided to try to run him off the road one day, and they got into a yelling match by the side of the road. I realized that he and Mutilate just might cancel each other out. I also realized I'd do best to focus on myself and my practice and not waste energy worrying about nasty colleagues. My best bet was to not be one.

Like clients, colleagues can also be good, bad or plain ugly. I try to give people the benefit of the doubt, but over the years, I have concluded that certain veterinarians can be some of the most unstable and unsavory human beings on the earth. My profession seems to have an inordinate number of toxic human beings masquerading as doctors. Yet when you look deeply into the life of an older veterinarian and at some of the clients who have warped him, you can understand what made him that way. And there, but for the grace of God, go all of us in this profession!

George had a string of encounters with a veterinarian who we've already met, a "Dr. Yesman." We both had a lot of dealings with him, each worse than the last. It was hard to imagine how someone like him had any clients at all, but if I've learned nothing else in private practice, I've learned these hard and fast rules:

1. The quality of medicine you practice has nothing to do with how much certain clients like you and remain loyal to you.
2. The personal morals that you embody have nothing to do with how much certain clients like you and remain loyal to you.
3. Reality and truth have nothing to do with how much certain clients like you and remain loyal to you.

This pendulum swings both ways. A client's loyalty can be as unfair and undeserved as another's criticism. Humans find their own truth and reality; changing this perception is practically impossible. Confucius said, "You can't teach a man what he thinks he already knows."

When George first arrived in Colorado, Dr. "Yesman" promptly told the town that George was an outlaw from Texas who had no vet license. For six months or so, George went about his business, ignorant of his outlaw status. Finally, a new client, impressed with his deft laceration repair skills, announced, "I don't care if you don't have a license, Dr. Platt! You're my new vet!"

To this day there are still people in the valley who believe that old Doc Platt was an unlicensed outlaw, and George saw no point in refuting them. He probably thought it was funny. I used to get more worked up about things like that than he did. He'd offer me helpful suggestions like, "Don't let 'em live rent-free in your head," "F**k 'em if they can't take a joke!" and my personal favorite, "Who gives a damn what she thinks? Hell, I wouldn't piss in her ear if her head was on fire!"

Dr. Yesman did take George's presence personally, and lost no opportunity to try to make George look bad. He was maniacally possessive of his clients, and if he thought any were defecting to George or me, he would call them obsessively and browbeat them over the phone. He was famous for just showing up and vaccinating "his" client's horses unscheduled, resulting in numerous double vaccinations if they had already scheduled George or me to do them.

We were treating a Friesian horse for a nasty parasite called ascarids, or roundworms. The horse had experienced an episode of abdominal pain, or "colic," and George had responded to the call. He had passed a stomach tube, a routine procedure on a colic, and was telling some off-colored joke when the horse strained slightly and a tangle of spaghetti-like worms flew out of the tube and landed on the ground.

The owner was horrified, pointing and spluttering at the wriggling mess. George glanced at the worms, calmly finished his joke, then looked at the end of the stomach tube where his mouth had recently been.

"Good thing I already had lunch, 'cause I'm pretty sure I just lost my appetite!"

Then he called me. "Didn't you just deworm this horse?!"

I had, two weeks ago.

"Well, you might want to tell the worms that. They don't seem to know that they're dead."

He put the horse on a very specific tapering deworming protocol. When you're treating a horse for a worm burden this large, you don't want to give a large dose and kill off the worms quickly, as they can cause a huge impaction. The owner and the barn staff were all on board with the treatment plan, and the infected horse was kept isolated from the rest of the herd.

A week later, the owner called, frantic.

"I was just told that Dr. Yesman was here this morning and vaccinated and dewormed my horse! Now he's colicking badly!"

I raced to the barn to find the poor Friesian on his side, thrashing. After a lot of drugs to ease his pain, several hours of monitoring, and IV fluids, he began to improve. Over the next 24 hours, he passed approximately 15 pounds of dead roundworms.

He survived the ordeal, but weeks later, it got back to me that Dr. Yesman was claiming that he had cured the horse by stepping in and giving the horse the full deworming dose, when George and I had been too scared to do so. The furious owner refused to pay Yesman's bill and he took her to collections. They ended up in court over it, and I do not know how it turned out. Interestingly, others rallied to his defense, crediting him with saving the horse.

On the same farm, I was called to see a horse with a cut leg. The client was one of Dr. Yesman's, but he was out of town, so I agreed to fill in until he returned. It was late evening, and the horse had knocked a small piece of skin from his lower leg. "Eloise," the client's trainer, was there glowering possessively at the wound, and Alberto, one of the barn workers, was holding the horse and glowering at Eloise. It was obvious that they were arguing about something.

After examination, it was clear that there was nothing to suture, so I cleaned and dressed the area, applying a thick leg wrap, and for good measure, started the horse on antibiotics. Eloise didn't say much as I handed the medicine to her. I left a message for Dr. Yesman, detailing the injury and my treatment. Eloise also called Dr. Yesman, appalled that I had not stitched this dreadful wound.

I rechecked the horse the next day, pleased at his progress. Another call to Dr. Yesman was ignored, but I left another long message and went home feeling happy about the whole thing.

At 8 p.m. my phone rang. It was the barn manager.

"Dr. Yesman and Eloise are here with the horse, and he's stitching up the leg!"

I was speechless. There was nothing to suture! What the hell was he doing?

Panting in indignation, I called George, and explained as fast as I could. "George, it's an abrasion! He's there right now sewing up a skin abrasion!"

George chuckled. "With what? Skin from Eloise's butt?"

That cheered me up, and soon we were onto other topics. George could always put things into perspective.

Several weeks later, the barn manager received a long letter from Dr. Yesman explaining why he should be put in charge of the entire barn. In the letter was an excerpt detailing my veterinary incompetence, "... as evidenced by the poor decision to leave a gaping wound unattended ..."

Nothing ever came of it, nor was Dr. Yesman "put in charge of the entire barn," but he continued to come and go until a year later when he managed to get himself banned from the premises entirely. Although Eloise stubbornly marched her client's horses half a mile to the public road to meet him, few others seemed so inclined, and they defected to George or me.

# An Anvil and an Opinion

*"The quickest way to piss off the self-appointed experts
is to use logic. They hate that."*
-George W Platt, DVM

"Make friends with the farriers, Courtney," George had said. This was easier said than done. It wasn't a problem for George, who'd had years of experience, solid credibility and had proven himself through his work with laminitic horses. I was fresh out of the gates, wet behind the ears, and not very impressive.

Farriers and vets don't always get along. The problems are deep-rooted and I have seen bad behavior from both professions. I'll never forget a shoer who wore a baseball hat with a picture of a horse foot in a circle, and a slash across the picture with a caption reading, "No Vets." He proudly wore this hat to a prominent vet clinic to consult with several respected veterinarians on a lameness problem with a horse he'd been shoeing, effectively killing any hope of good communication. On the flip side, I've seen veterinarians embarrass themselves trying to tell a good farrier how to do his job and I've also been one of those veterinarians. Like I said, it goes both ways.

In Great Britain, there are high standards for Farriers, the professional term for a horseshoer who has gone through the proper training. The profession of farriery is regulated in England, Wales and Scotland by the Farriers Registration Council (FRC). Farriers complete a four-year and two-month Advanced Apprenticeship in Farriery, including 23 weeks at college. They must become registered before they are allowed to practice on horses. In addition to the college and apprenticeship training requirements, a variety of additional diplomas and specific certifications must be obtained to become a registered farrier in Great Britain.

There is a regulatory council to which concerns and complaints regarding illegal horseshoers and registered farriers can be submitted. Registered farriers hold their profession in high regard and maintain rigorous standards. Illegal farriers are reported and can be prosecuted, and clients who use an illegal farrier can be implicated for "aiding and abetting a criminal act."

In the U.S., the term "farrier" has become diluted by a sea of horseshoers with various and often dubious standards for claiming the title. In the U.S., anyone with an anvil and an opinion can set themselves up as a farrier. The title now appears to include the backyard shoer, weekend internet course attendee, the guy who studied with Dad, who also had no formal training, and the fad and pseudo-science shoers arriving with their own set of "certifications." The farrier profession is not regulated in America and no legal certification currently exists.

There is a group of professional farriers who have voluntarily worked hard to master standards recognized by three organizations in the U.S.: the American Farrier's Association, the Guild of Professional Farriers and the Brotherhood of Working Farriers. These men and women attain voluntary certifications within these organizations and maintain them with annual continuing education, attending conferences, working with peers, and deepening their understanding of a science that has been around since the Roman Empire.

The AFA's program is the largest with close to 3,000 certified farriers. Additionally, the AFA program has a reciprocity agreement with the Farrier Registration Council and the Worshipful Company of Farriers in the UK. The AFA standards are high and the certifications are rigorous.

Unfortunately there is often little reward for the professional farrier in the U.S. who maintains his standards and certifications. With no one to defend him or help uphold his hard-won credentials, he has to compete with a barrage of questionably trained lay-shoers who are legally undercutting his prices and simultaneously blowing established shoeing standards and farrier science out the window.

We all know shoers who are not certified who do a good job. There are several in my area that I work with regularly, and they are very skilled. But how do we differentiate the good from the bad if they are not certified? The public becomes the judge of the lay-shoers, rather than a board of their peers, and this is where the trouble starts.

The court of horse owner opinion, swayed by popularity, rumor and myth, is a dangerous judge, and becomes fueled by its own power. And when little Prima decides that a pseudoscience shoeing fad has made her chronically lame show horse into a chronically lame champion that isn't lame even though he's lame, suddenly a stampede of her ladies are insisting that this type of shoeing is the greatest thing in the world and woe to anyone who doesn't immediately fire their old farrier and leap onto the bandwagon.

The fired farrier watches his carefully tended feet morph into rippled distortions with squared toes, and gets to hear the owner squealing about how great their horse is now doing, even though there is initially zero difference in the way the horse is moving. The fired farrier now gets blamed for every performance issue under the sun, whether or not it was present when he started shoeing the horse, and the barn sighs in relief to finally have an "expert" working on their horses.

Under the care of the new "expert" pseudo-shoer, the toes run farther and farther out in front with under-run heels, bowed quarters and dorsal hoof wall cracks. Horses aren't performing well, but owners have now become diagnosticians, blaming saddles, teeth, and negative auras. Prima is peddling her Natural Supplements like crazy, treating liver congestion, and detoxifying the immune system. Shoes are thrown and have to be replaced by the local farriers, who frown at the condition of the foot and wonder why they're good enough to tack a shoe back on but are not allowed to trim and balance the whole horse. In six months or so when the bloom has left the rose, the owners start to wonder why the feet don't look quite right, and their horse still isn't performing as well as they'd been promised, and they decide to look for yet another shoer.

The real farriers assess the situation and realize immediately what they are up against. They now have to try to turn around a situation that has run amok for months. Any horse professional can tell you that months of poor shoeing is difficult to correct, cannot be fixed in one visit, and that sometimes the horse will get worse for a while. Lacking an educated clientele, the professional farrier struggles for several months to bring the feet back into balance while the owners, wanting to ride, drum their fingers and wonder why this is taking so long.

Enter the veterinarian. This can go one of two ways.

Scenario 1: A veterinarian is called because the horse is lame and is given no shoeing history because the owner has no idea that this could be related to the "performance issues". The vet forgets to ask about shoeing history, and the farrier is not there to elaborate because he wasn't invited.

The vet watches the horse go, lunges him in circles, hoof tests him, maybe nerve blocks him, takes a bazillion X-rays, doesn't find an obvious cause of lameness, and decides to plunk down a shoeing "prescription." It reads, "Increase breakover and elevate the heels with a 3-degree wedge pad." If quizzed, it is unlikely that he could define "breakover" or specify exactly how he would like the farrier to achieve this, or why. He will never speak directly to the farrier, instead pointing out all sorts of things that he doesn't like about the feet to the owner, getting her upset, and leaving the owner to tell the farrier how to shoe the horse.

The farrier, already frustrated by lack of respect for his abilities and lack of appreciation for what he's been trying to fix, reads the shoeing prescription in disgust and expresses contempt for the veterinarian. The farrier has been trying to address months of damage caused by poor shoeing. He knows perfectly well that the feet are not what they should be. He's trying to bring the foot back underneath the horse and correct the underrun heels and distorted hoof capsule, and is now effectively being asked to crush the heels further under a wedge pad and slice off what little remains of the toe. His name will be on this "prescription" work, a detail often disregarded by the veterinarian.

Maybe the farrier reluctantly goes along with it and nails on the requisite wedge and rolls the toe, doing the best he can. Thanks to the vet's comments, the owner has lost confidence in the farrier, and secretly wonders if perhaps she should try to find someone else. When the horse is no better in a few weeks, as there was no actual diagnosis made by the veterinarian, suddenly the farrier finds himself replaced. Maybe he got a phone call to let him know, or maybe he just showed up and saw a new person working on what used to be his client's horse. He and the vet never did speak directly, and his resentment toward veterinarians increases. Meanwhile, the horse, that is the real victim, gets worse.

Scenario 2: A veterinarian is called because the horse is lame and is given no shoeing history because the owner has no idea that this could be related to the lameness. The veterinarian speaks with the owner over the phone, asking detailed questions about the horse's history and shoeing. The vet then calls the farrier before coming out and the farrier provides as much history as possible. The vet expresses understanding for the position the farrier has been in, and they agree to meet and look at the horse together.

The vet now has a better comprehension of the situation and is unlikely to view the farrier as an adversary. The farrier appreciates being consulted and treated as a professional instead of disposable help, and is unlikely to view the vet as an adversary. They realize that the owner is uneducated and they understand that by presenting a united front as two professionals working as a team, they are more likely to be effective in helping the horse.

The vet can help educate the owner, and support the farrier in the process of turning the feet around. The farrier can continue to do his job in a supportive environment, rather than a mistrustful one. The horse will benefit the most from the cooperation. Should a specific shoeing need be determined during the diagnostics and radiographs, the vet and the farrier will approach it together.

So in the U.S., where there is no regulation of farriers and no set of universal standards that shoers must follow, how is one to know a good farrier from a bad shoer? As a sidenote, vets are regulated, licensed and have to complete continuing education classes to keep their licenses current, yet some of these licensed veterinarians are the worst practitioners out there. So how can one know the difference between a good vet and a bad vet?

# The Barefoot Wars

*Client: "My horse is still lame."*

*Me: "He needs an MRI so that we can accurately diagnose the problem. Remember we discussed that last week?"*

*Client: "I was reading on the internet. Oh what's it called.....mustang swoop. No, roll. Mustang roll."*

*Me: "That's a type of trim...."*

*Client: "MUSTANG ROLL!"*

*Me: "Well, the problem isn't in the foot. It's in his ankle which is above the foot. Remember when we did the nerve blocks to figure out where he was sore?"*

*Client: "Well it said that lameness is caused because of shoes. And he has shoes on!"*

*Me: "What said that?"*

*Client: "The website! And we have to do a MUSTANG ROLL!"*

*Me: "But the problem isn't in the foot. And I work on a lot of sound horses who wear horseshoes. Lameness is not caused because of shoes."*

*Client: "Well, I need a new farrier who will do the swoop.... I mean roll."*

*Me: "Uh....."*

*Client: "Have you heard of Evelyn "Soaring Eagle Wind" McClowski? She can swoop the feet."*
*Me: "No, I can't say that I have."*
*Client: "I'm calling her." [glares suspiciously at me as though I'm trying to pull a fast one]*
*Me: "Fine then."*
*Client: "I'll let you know how it goes with the eagle roll. I mean mustang roll."*
*Me: "Yes."*

Lameness in the riding horse can be one of the most frustrating events that a horse owner will face during their equine-owning tenure. While some lameness problems are very simple and easily fixed, soreness in the horse can be difficult and sometimes impossible to diagnose, becoming costly, time consuming, and chronic. Lameness issues can also challenge the relationship between the veterinarians, farrier and horse owner like no other.

A client once asked George to name the most common cause of injury to the horse. George looked at her without a hint of irony and replied, "Air". Very simply, some horses just seem hell-bent on destroying themselves and there is a funny image of a horse swaddled in bubble wrap being circulated on the internet, titled, "My Horse's New Turnout Gear."

When I am contacted by an owner about a lame horse, my anxiety levels increase before I've even seen the animal, as my relationship with my client is likely to undergo a significant challenge if I cannot fix the problem quickly. A lame horse generates angst in the barn, and the owner, worried and surrounded by advice-offering friends can become extremely volatile. It is tempting to begin the conversation with the client by saying, "Hi, this is Dr. Diehl and it is not my fault that your horse is lame. How can I help you?"

The best possible lameness case is an easily diagnosed problem, a treatment plan, and a sound horse within one to two weeks. These cases make the vet a hero. We swoop in, work our magic, hand over our remedies, and presto, the horse is cured! Hoof abscesses, bruises, small infected cuts and mild sprains usually fall into this category.

Almost as desirable is the lameness that defies diagnostics but resolves after resting the horse and prescribing some anti-inflammatories and topical poultices for a few weeks. Some vets will take all of the credit for fixing the horse even though they didn't exactly know what was causing the lameness, but George would say, "That horse got well in spite of us, not because of us!" And I have no problem admitting that to the owner. Taking credit for the body healing itself is a slippery slope, as there will be times when the body doesn't heal itself. Then what?

Everyone loves it when the horse heals quickly. It's even better if the owner goes out of town and the horse is cured when they return, and you don't have to endure them drumming their fingers and wondering if "we" shouldn't be trying another "therapy" that they read about on the internet or heard about in the barn that might coincidentally coordinate with time of healing and be given all of the credit for "fixing" the horse.

Not included in this chapter are readily diagnosed torn tendons, bone chips in joints, fractures, and ligament injuries. They come with a clear set of directives and often involve referral, so owner compliance is usually easily obtained. These cases do not apply to this discussion.

What you are going to encounter in the next storyline is what I refer to as the Scenario of Doom. This refers to the lameness case that you and your colleagues cannot completely diagnose that does not respond quickly or well to any treatments provided. The Scenario of Doom will hit every few years, leaving the beleaguered veterinarian and farrier emotionally battered by the irate client and her friends. Often you both lose the client when she goes off the deep end and hauls in the witchdoctors.

Very simply there are soft-tissue and skeletal injuries that your x-ray and ultrasound units cannot detect. There are horses that are sore in multiple places in their bodies yet established diagnostic tests cannot pinpoint the problem. There are back and pelvic problems and chronic ligament, tendon and joint issues that will defy most conventional approaches. And there are horses that will remain chronically lame despite our best efforts and can only be helped by prolonged rest or full retirement.

Owners can spend tens of thousands of dollars pursuing costly tests and procedures, only to end up with a pricey, well-injected, well-medicated, well-discussed, lame horse. Add in an unhealthy, anthropomorphic attachment of the owner to her "husband-substitute" horse, and the luckless vet and farrier who cannot fix the lameness are going to bear the brunt of their client's wrath.

In Act 1 of the Scenario of Doom, the farrier and the veterinarian have probably been working on the horse together. The hours they spend in the barn resetting shoes, staring at x-rays, and reassuring the owner are overshadowed by the hours that are spent researching texts, consulting with colleagues and lying awake at night fretting over the case. Neither will be compensated for these lost hours.

The owner is usually present for the reset shoes, the repeated x-rays and the recheck exams of the horse's gaits. Maybe you remind her that the horse was lame when she purchased it. Maybe the lameness is improving slowly, maybe not, but the owner's frustration is increasing. The whispering in the barn is also gaining momentum as other boarders discuss the horse that the ignorant vet and farrier just can't fix.

After several resets without measurable improvement, the situation becomes precarious. People in the barn are openly offering their own diagnoses of the problem and recommending other treatment methods and at this point the owner is beginning to doubt the vet and the farrier. She may stick with them for another few weeks, but the stage is already being set up for the next scene.

In Scenario of Doom, Act 2, you'll arrive at the barn one day and see an SUV parked in front of the sliding door, boasting a sign that reads, "Dreamcatcher Spirit Wind Natural Wild Barefoot Trims". With a sinking feeling in your stomach, you enter the barn.

You're greeted by a hefty middle-aged woman wearing a bandanna tied around her head, large jeans, a flowered button down shirt and hiking boots. She's wearing gardening gloves and carrying a plastic bucket of farrier tools, a bag of horse treats and is wearing an immaculate shoeing apron. You'll notice that she's already pulled the shoes off of your patient and is explaining something at top speed to a rapt owner who is nodding happily. If you can get a word in edgewise, which is unlikely, she'll either ask you loaded questions with well-rehearsed answers that she'll provide, or she'll use a lot of fad lingo that refers to nothing scientific.

Her background is sketchy, but you manage to learn that this is her third career, the first two having nothing to do with horses. At age 46, she got her very first horse, a lame horse rescued from the racetrack. She named him "Dreamcatcher Spirit Wind" and "cured" him with her hoof trimming skills after vets diagnosed him with a chronic disease of his feet. She tells you eagerly that she went on the internet to help Dreamcatcher after being told that he'd never be sound, and had the good fortune to meet a barefoot trimmer who explained that the horseshoes were the root of all evil, and that the horse had to be maintained barefoot like the wild horses. After some intense animal communication in which Dreamcatcher Spirit Wind revealed that he wept in grief whenever he saw the farrier pull up to his stall, she became a barefoot trimmer.

You swallow hard, picturing the thin soled, crummy feet of the typical racetrack Thoroughbred, who is about as far removed from a wild horse as a dachshund is from a wolf, and you ask her what she means by "cured". She tells you happily that while her horse can't be ridden because of the mental trauma he'd suffered, he is cantering around in his paddock now, when he only used to trot. She'll go on to tell you that horses must be maintained on pea gravel and fed "salads" to stay healthy, and within several minutes she has prescribed several books written by laymen that you simply must read, as they'll show you just how much you don't know about the horse's foot.

She's also a Homeopathic Healer, you learn, and she tucks several white tablets called "Nux Vomit" or something similar, into the horse's mouth to be dissolved "under the tongue". If the horse spits them out, she explains that he absorbed what he needed and "shed" what he didn't. You have a momentary flashback to an expensive injection that you once gave to a horse that ended up spraying the wall, your face and the grumpy owner's jacket and you imagine trying to explain to him that the horse must have "shed" what he didn't need.

You'll listen in amazement as the trimmer verbally violates known and established horseshoeing principles, flooding your ears with terms like, "natural balance", "Mustang roll", "white-line-strategy trim", "pooled bars", "detoxification of the pumps" and other such mysteries. Then she becomes a veterinary expert, explaining that the lines in the feet tell her that the horse suffers from a stressed liver, congestion of the immune system and chronic kidney pain. Everyone is now satisfied that the kidneys are causing the horse's lameness and your credibility has effectively been blown out the window.

As she nips away bits of the hoof wall, she shows her audience how she is allowing the "detoxified mustang inside" to come out and join the world. The teary eyed owner and her friends, hands clasped, hang on every word, and somewhere, a wooden flute begins to play.

Since you have now been rendered extraneous, invisible and incredibly uneducated, the best thing to do is fake an emergency and get the hell out of there. Don't argue, debate, protest or otherwise engage with this situation. You will not succeed with these people.

Over the next 10-12 weeks, several scenarios are possible, the most likely being that the horse stays exactly at the same level of lameness but no one except you and the fired farrier recognize this. And every time you enter the barn, the Nux Vomit-infused horse is paraded in front of you so that you can marvel at "how free he is in the shoulder, how improved his break-over is, and how soft and happy his eye has become". You could point out that there is absolutely no change in the lameness, and you'd be correct, but since they've already decided that he's "better", good luck with that.

The second likely possibility is that the horse is worse. Naturally the trimmer will have an explanation for this pre-programmed into the owner's brain, and if you point out your concern to the owner, she'll interrupt you with a canned monologue about how horseshoes caused "atrophy" of the feet, and destruction of the hoof tubules and this soreness is part of the healing process as the foot has to regrow all of the structures that were slaughtered by the shoes. As the owner's mouth moves, you sense a bandana-wearing woman with gardening gloves bellowing at you. And you as a DVM have completely and utterly failed the horse by allowing the tissue-trashing horseshoes to be nailed on in the first place. Somewhere, Dreamcatcher is shaking his mane in sorrow at your ignorance.

You could try to argue. You could name hundreds of shod horses whose feet have not been murdered by shoes and you could explain how barefoot horses often erode their unprotected feet into painful nubs on rough terrain. You could comment that Veterinary and Farrier Science would probably take notice of chronic and widespread "crippling" of horses with shoes, and enact a policy change. But you can see that you'd be talking to yourself. The only thing you're teaching the owner at this point is that you and the fired farrier are unenlightened foot assassins, conspiring to cripple as many horses as possible before retirement.

In a rare scenario the horse may show some slight improvement, so naturally all of the credit goes to the Wild Barefoot Mustang Natural Dreamcatcher Detoxifying Trim. The logic here is that since Event "B" followed Event "A" that "A" (the trim) caused "B" (the improvement). You naively give this one a good fight. You point out that if you shake your fist at the sky and then it thunders, chances are good that you didn't actually make it thunder. You name other factors in the "A" group, like time, rest, drugs, and time. But your words fall on deaf ears. The trim is fixing the horse, not any of these other factors and that is the end of it. Go away, vet.

It's a frustrating place to end up. As annoying as I found these situations to be, I'd learned to let them go. There wasn't much that I could do to change the dynamic, and initially I did try to reason with the owners and the trimmers. But I learned that as soon as I stopped talking, things would go right back to rampant superstition which was apparently way more fun to believe.

But I wasn't the only person getting their toes tromped on by these trimmers.

One day, I arrived at a big barn noting with interest that the Dreamcatcher Wild Natural SUV was blocked in by a huge Dodge truck with a Stonewell aluminum insert on the back, a rifle rack on the rear window and "CJF" (Certified Journeyman Farrier) painted on the side in huge letters. The forge inside the Stonewell was on, sending a clear message that the truck wasn't going to move anytime soon.

It didn't take me long to find them. The trimmer, who obviously had arrived first, was red faced and puffing with only one foot trimmed on her patient, and the CJF had dragged his anvil as close as he could and was fiercely hammering away, sweat pouring down his face. An athletic looking quarter horse waited nearby, held by a well-known and successful trainer.

I noticed that every time the trimmer started to talk, the furious hammering would increase in intensity and drown her out, sparks flying every which way. The farrier made brisk laps to his truck, brandishing red hot shoes on his return as he marched right between the trimmer and her patient. She stomped over to him and his horse, waving her arms and mouthing words and he grinned and applied the searing hot shoe to the bottom of the horse's foot. Spluttering, the woman disappeared into a blue cloud of smoke, the top of her bandanna barely visible.

Within 25 minutes the farrier had shod the entire horse and another one was being led up to him. Standing too close, the trimmer wiped her face and made a loud comment about hoof butchers and how sad it was for the poor horses. The farrier seemed to ignore her, but suddenly a red hot shoe tumbled from his anvil, forcing her to leap out of the way. He gave her a delighted grin, apologized, and captured the shoe deftly, commencing his loud hammering.

The woman gave up and returned to her patient. She labored to finish the second foot and was breathing so hard that her face had gone a dull purple. She had to keep setting the foot down and straightening up, hand on the small of her back. The farrier had shod three horses by the time she finally finished with her patient, and had packed up and departed before she even realized he'd parked her in.

Although she stuck it out for a while and showed up at various barns in the area, she didn't last at any of them and eventually I stopped seeing her SUV around town. Weeks later, I couldn't help but notice that many of the "Wild Natural Dreamcatcher Mustang" feet were wearing horseshoes again.

The "wild horse" analogy is a poor one, as there are no true wild horses anymore. What we have are herds of feral horses, animals descended from domestic stock that were left to survive on their own. Any BLM official can tell you that some feral horses have terrible hoof problems too- their "wild" status does not automatically grant them perfect feet.

For the record, I have absolutely no problem with barefoot horses. If a horse can remain sound without horseshoes, so be it. However, a regular farrier is perfectly capable of trimming the foot properly if he knows the horse will not be shod. There is no magical way to trim a foot, and if the horse is ever sore after a trimming, something is wrong.

# George

Diehl and Platt attempting to jam on the banjo and dobro, 2005

George deserves his own book and one day I will write it. Suffice it to say that George was the antidote to everything that I hated about my profession and some of the clients that I had to deal with. Being with George kept me focused on the important things. We were there to help horses. I'll never forget his patented dismissals of someone he didn't like. He'd say, "They don't care about horses!"

He used to say, "This whole ship'll be yours someday, Courtney," meaning that I was to carry on with our mission after he was gone. I couldn't fathom that someday there would be no George. He was larger than life. Unstoppable. And his work with laminitis had been groundbreaking, yet the vet schools just weren't on board with his methods. He called them "Bute lovers," and was very disappointed in his alma mater for the way they were treating laminitis cases.

George supported my decisions, even if he didn't agree with them. He didn't speak to me for six months when he learned that I was taking a course in Veterinary Chiropractic, as he loathed the field. But he got over it. He was there on my wedding day, bandages on his hands from a horse that'd kicked him, and he played his beloved Dobro in celebration. The following year when I told him that I was pregnant with my first child, he groaned and complained that he'd never get to retire, then hugged me tight and told me that hard work was good for pregnant women.

It was a tough day when I had to tell George that I was selling my practice and leaving for Kentucky. I'd gotten accepted for a fellowship position in Internal Medicine and Critical Care, in a large equine hospital in Lexington, and it was time to go shake up my brain and learn some new things. George understood. He always did. We had dinner a few weeks before we left, my 4-day-old baby balanced on the table, and Cornelia turned to me.

"How on earth are you going to look after that baby when you're at the hospital all the time?"

I smiled at Jim. He winked at me, ready for his new role as stay-at-home dad. We had some major changes coming our way but we were ready for them. We were excited to leave for Kentucky, but I hated to leave George.

We talked for a long time after the meal was over, then

inevitably the phone rang, and George rose to answer it. He was gone for a while, then returned, his face grim.

"Sherri Gilkerson was killed today. Crushed by a horse."

Sherri was a lovely young horse trainer who both of us had worked for. Although George was her number one vet, she'd always been gracious and kind to me when I'd worked with her, and I'd liked her a lot. She'd moved to Arizona and apparently had been holding a horse for a veterinarian when the accident happened.

I thought of all of the times a horse that I'd been working on had acted similarly, putting me and the handler at risk. We had a hushed conversation about the dangers involved with working with horses, then George fell silent, staring at the wall.

That ended the evening, and George bid me a brief goodnight, tears on his cheeks. We left for Kentucky two weeks later.

The fellowship was grueling as promised, and I didn't see my family very often. I was trying to nurse my baby throughout the hard work, and I brought a pump to the hospital, thinking I could keep up that way. The hospital was accommodating, finding me a supply closet next to the hyperbaric oxygen chamber where I could pump undisturbed. Staff was warned to not be alarmed if Dr. Diehl suddenly emerged from the closet at odd times bearing plastic baggies.

The reality was that a nursing mother needs to pump every two hours, and as hard as I tried, that was impossible when the hospital was busy. I was crushed when my husband told me that he had to buy formula to feed our daughter, but knew that it was inevitable. My husband deserved an award for all that he did at home while I was completing the fellowship.

I learned amazing things while I was there. Procedures that I'd never even seen performed became routine to me. I could now handle cases that would have terrified me and sent me scrambling for the phone to refer the horse. I was flying high with all the new knowledge. But I didn't see any improvement over the way George was treating his laminitis cases.

The hospitalized horses with laminitis were medicated heavily, remained standing on their ice-booted feet, and many became sinkers. One of my jobs was to take X-rays each day, measuring the degree of the sinking. Everyone would say that it was too bad – we'd done everything we could. I could hear George insisting, "Let them lay down, put heart bar shoes on them to support the bone, get them off the damn Bute!" I called him many nights in tears after having euthanized yet another sinker case. I tried to respectfully share his methods with the hospital, but I received only polite stares and a dismissal. I was told that, "We don't shoe acute laminitis cases."

I found it hard to respond to that without being contradictory, but George and I had shod every single acute laminitis case that we'd treated. And they all got well. Why was this so hard for others to see! George even came to Kentucky to speak at the Kentucky Horseshoeing School, a mere five minutes from the hospital. I invited everyone to attend his talk. Not one person went.

I will always be grateful for the experience in Kentucky. I learned a lot in the six months that I was there, and worked with some of the best doctors in the country. I learned a great deal about where my own strengths and weaknesses were, and I saw that I had a great deal of room for improvement in many areas. At many levels, I was taken apart and put back together, and overall, it was humbling and life-changing to be a part of the experience there.

But the main thing that I learned was that George's methods for treating laminitis were completely effective. His cases got well if he could get to them before the drugs. I saw it firsthand and I will never forget how it felt to watch a horse become a sinker when I knew there was a better way. I wanted to show the hospital George's way but not one person wanted to hear about it. Instead I gave the drugs, iced the feet, took the X-rays and euthanized the horses.

After a year of travel and experiencing different places,

we returned to Colorado, and I devoted myself to learning George's laminitis protocols with renewed energy. Now that I'd seen what the rest of the world was doing, I was even more committed to treating them his way.

Jim and I had spent months researching areas to start a new practice when we returned to Colorado. It's not easy to find the right place. You don't want an overpopulation of vets, as there is only so much work to go around, but you would like to have a good quality of life and live in a beautiful area. You also need an area that is fairly economically stable with plenty of horses to work on.

We had researched many areas to set up a practice and had rejected all of them. Either there were not enough horses or there were too many vets. I had called every vet in every area that I could find, and if they told me that I would hurt their business by showing up, I crossed that area off my list.

Just as my husband and I were giving up hope, we looked at Friendlytown, Colorado. The vets that I spoke with told us that there was room for us. It was a real town, offered all the things that we loved to do, and there were lots of horses. We arrived with our 2-year-old daughter, took a gamble on a large business loan and set up my new practice.

George would make the drive to Friendlytown regularly as I called him in on every single laminitis case that I saw. He also taught me how to geld horses standing, a procedure I'd always watched with envy. Under George's watchful eye, I resected feet, checked the sizing and fit of the heart bar shoe, radiographed feet and removed testicles.

Right after starting up my practice, the economy took a huge nosedive, and I learned that I was pregnant with my second child. I had worked all through my first pregnancy and everything had been fine, so I figured I'd make it work somehow. Initially the calls were slow to come in, but overall the first year was solid and my husband and I were feeling good about the new area. Meanwhile my abdomen was expanding.

I needed maternity Carhartts and no one carried them, or, for that matter, any sort of work dungaree for the pregnant vet. All I could find were foolish little khaki lounging pants with delicate little pockets, perhaps for a bon bon or two. Now I knew I wasn't the only pregnant woman who had to work for a living. Where were women finding their maternity work clothes?

We solved the problem by taking two of my favorite pairs of Carhartts to a seamstress friend of mine and having her convert them into maternity pants for me. I alternated the two pairs for the remainder of my pregnancy, and despite the countless washings, they survived.

Working an active job while pregnant was interesting. Again, I am only one of many who have worked through a pregnancy, so I am not unique. I will say that it gave me the opportunity to develop strengths that I didn't know I had, and I am definitely a lifetime member of the sisterhood of working pregnant women.

My doctor cleared me to do activities that I had done before my pregnancy. This included chiropractic work on horses, limb flexion tests, radiology, and palpating mares. My belly got in the way on occasion, but for the most part, I was able to work unhindered. There were a few memorable moments though.

For example, did you know that your second pregnancy is more uncomfortable than your first? Initially I thought I was just getting older. After all I was 39, and things just seemed harder, my body slower that I remembered.  But apparently the ligaments that support the uterus get stretched out during your first baby, and are more sensitive to weight and pressure, leaving you with a constant dull ache in your lower belly. Because the top of the pregnant uterus compresses your stomach and diaphragm, shortness of breath and acid reflux are daily realities.

Another fun thing to know about your second pregnancy is the sad fact that the urethral sphincter, involved in bladder control, isn't as effective as it once was. Don't laugh too hard, enter a coughing fit, or gag unexpectedly. There are consequences. Keep a change of clothes in the truck!

The clients worried more about me than I did. I'd be stitching up a laceration, and the rule of horse lacerations are that they never occur in convenient locations on the horse's body, and I'd look up to see the client offering a chair, a glass of iced tea, a sandwich. They'd hover over me sometimes holding my arm or putting a hand on my shoulder.

I remember one call in particular. The laceration was low on the horse's side, and I had to bend way over to pull it together. I'd straighten up periodically and stretch my lower back like a pregnant woman does, and each time I did this, the client would panic, thinking I was going into labor. I lost track of the number of times I said, "I'm fine."

I admit I didn't feel great half the time, but if I stayed home how would the bills get paid? I was planning to have a home delivery and had started meeting with the midwife regularly. When my due date was a few weeks away, she banned me from leaving the area, making me promise never to travel more than 20 minutes away. I had an assistant with me most days, so stupidly I ignored the travel restrictions.

On my last day of real calls, we had traveled 70 miles to take some X-rays on a horse's foot at George's request, as he couldn't get there for several weeks. He would have understood if I'd declined, but foolishly I agreed to go. The drive seemed to take forever and lifting the equipment out of the truck was harder than normal. I had to stop and rest in between trips. When I bent over to shoot the X-rays, my belly cramped hard and I blacked out briefly and had to kneel down until I could see again.

My assistant and the client were at my side quickly. I insisted I was fine, went on to take the worst X-rays of my career, and we packed up and headed back home. Nothing more happened on the drive, and it was another week before my daughter made her arrival, but it was an overdue wake-up call for me to be more careful. Going into early labor on a faraway ranch would not be good. I changed the message on my machine to let clients know that I would be on limited availability.

I did a few more local calls but kept them simple. The last week of my pregnancy was uneventful, and my daughter was born at home, the way we planned. I went back to work four days after she was born, and she came on calls with me. I tried to keep my schedule light, but it was July in the horse world, and a lot of work was coming in. I wasn't trying to be superwoman, but I still needed to earn a living, and maternity leave was not something we could afford.

Clients were amused when I entered the barn with a baby in a carrier. We slung the carrier from stall doors, perched it on the back of the vet unit, balanced it on tables in the barns. My favorite resting place was a clean galvanized garbage can. The carrier fit perfectly into the opening, and my daughter was at a perfect height to see everything. Plus it wouldn't tip over. I could work, take a break to nurse the baby and change diapers, or even better, hand the baby to a visiting grandmother on the farm.

One client teased me that the baby gave me an unfair advantage over the other vets in the area, and that people called me just so they could hold the baby. I joked back that I already had another one on the way just to keep the advantage going. I once tried to make a list of everyone in the county who had held my daughter, and I ran out of space on the paper.

My daughter came on calls with me until she was about 4 months old. We decided to get an au pair to be at home with the girls so I could continue to work full time. While I missed having her with me, it did make life easier to be able to leave her home, and it was better for her too. It was a sweet but strange chapter in my life, and I am glad that I have a lot of pictures of those days. I am also glad that I will never, ever do that again!

In 2010, George was invited to speak at the American Farrier's Convention in Portland, Oregon. He kindly invited me to be his co-speaker. I was going to discuss the heart bar shoe applications for navicular syndrome, another foot problem, and George would present the laminitis portion.

One week before we were due to get on a plane, George had a skiing accident on Vail Mountain, giving himself a severe concussion. His helmet was broken and he was unconscious when ski patrol found him. He was awake by the time they got him down, but he couldn't remember his street address or phone number.

He called me that night, sounding frail, and tried to explain what had happened, but he was very confused. I figured that was it for the conference, but I forgot that it was George W. Platt that I was talking to. Confused as he might have been, he wasn't that confused. In a firm voice, he announced that he was going to Oregon no matter what. Then in a weaker voice, he suggested that it might be good if I sat next to him onstage to prompt him.

I was suffering from vertigo after a nasty strep throat infection and was experiencing nausea and dizziness. We were going to be quite the pair, George and I, the vets from Colorado. I'd fall off the stage and George would forget where it was! And there were going to be 300-400 people in the audience!

We made it to Oregon and completed our presentation with a few glitches, but overall it went well. George was not himself, but he stayed on track and completed his portion just fine. Those of us who had heard him give his talk multiple times noticed that his storytelling was subdued, but he got all of his points across well. There was a line of farriers waiting for his autograph when we got to the exhibit hall.

# The Last Colic

Diehl and Platt, 2005

Over the next six months, George's mental function went into a decline. He didn't regain the ground he'd lost after the crash, and seemed to be getting worse at times. He called me one day to announce his retirement from vet practice, something I'd seen coming, but still wasn't quite prepared for. He called me a lot during these days, and I still think of all of the times I was too busy to pick up the phone to talk to my friend who was home alone, bored out of his mind.

I stopped in to see him whenever I was in Eagle, and one day in spring I dragged him out on a few calls when my truck broke down. His vet truck was half empty when he picked me up, so I grabbed what we needed from mine before the tow truck took it away and we tore off down the road like old times, headed to a colic, Dolly Parton blaring from the tinny speakers.

But it wasn't the same. George talked a lot, at times forgetting who I was and where we were going. I had to give him directions to a farm that he'd been to dozens of times. He told stories of his past, stories I'd never heard before, and I remained quiet and let him talk. Once he looked at me, desolation on his face, and said, "Courtney, I hate this. I hate it." I knew what he meant, but all I could do was squeeze his arm and tell him it would be OK.

When we got to the colicking horse, however, Dr. Platt took one look, sprang from the truck and was all business. Once again, he exploded into action, and in short order had examined the sick horse, performed a rectal exam and passed a stomach tube, this last move amazing the owners as the horse was violently head shy and dangerous to handle. Dr. Platt was in full command of the situation, and very soon was pumping fluid from his bucket into the horse's stomach.

"Dr. Platt, what are you giving him?" asked the owner, a petite woman in a tennis dress and a sun visor.

"Mag sulfate," said George, pumping furiously.

"And oil?" she said.

"Heck, no. There's no oil in there! Just plain mag sulfate and water!"

"And what does that do?" asked the lady pleasantly.

George stopped pumping and leered at her wickedly. He

winked at me, then announced, "It's gonna make him shit from here to the truck!"

The horse made a full recovery, and immensely pleased with himself, Dr. Platt drove us home without a trace of confusion. We spent the evening at his house looking at slides of various foot problems and strange diseases of horses. I remember sitting at his dining room table and feeling like everything before me was passing by quickly, and that I didn't have much time left with George and Cornelia.

The next day I filled out the paperwork nominating George for the Colorado Veterinary Medical Association's Distinguished Service Award. I got several of his colleagues to write letters of recommendation, and it was a unanimous decision by the committee to give him the award, which would be presented at the September 2011 conference in Loveland, Colorado.

He was proud when he got the news, and I called to congratulate him. He was abrupt on the phone, and more confused than normal. I told him that I was so proud of him, and that I'd be in the audience cheering as he went up to receive his award. His voice sounded shaky as he told me goodbye.

That was the last time I spoke to him. George suffered a massive stroke a week later and was rushed to Denver. Although he stabilized and seemed to show signs of improvement initially, by the time I got to Denver to see him, he was unresponsive.

He languished in the stroke unit, and was there when the CVMA conference began. I went to the awards ceremony and received his award for him, knowing in my heart that he'd never wake up to see it. They took him to surgery, moved him to ICU, then finally to hospice. On September 21, 2011, George Walter Platt, DVM passed away, his family by his side.

# The Big One

There were dozens of times after George died when I caught myself picking up the phone to ask him a question, run a case by him, lean on him after a tough run-in with a nasty client. I'd have his number halfway dialed before I remembered that I couldn't call him anymore. I knew eventually that I was going to get a monster case that I needed his help on and that he wouldn't be there to help me anymore. And one day, in September 2012, almost exactly a year after his death, that case arrived, the laminitis case that would change me forever.

To me, the definition of a great client is one who trusts me to do my job, asks intelligent questions, ignores fads or trends, and pays their bills promptly. I have been blessed with many such people in my life, and they provide balm for a spirit wounded by Prima or Jessamine dealings. When you work with a great client, it's as easy as breathing. It makes you realize how much unnecessary nonsense you have to put up with sometimes. It puts everything into perspective.

This story is about a great client named Wendy Parker and her horse Ghost. I'd been Ghost's vet for 12 years and he and I had a relationship built on tolerance for one another, but little else. We had an agreement, Ghost and I. He would refrain from hitting me in the head with his big skull, and I would refrain from seizing him by the nose. Ghost would allow me to float his teeth, vaccinate him and perform general vet duties on him, but in general he was not a warm and fuzzy horse.

With his family, Ghost was a machine. He carried his riders through ropings, barrel races and gymkanas, and was one of the fastest 4H horses around. So fast, in fact, that he was evicted from the "slower" horse shows. Everyone knew and admired Ghost and his athletic talents.

One September morning, Wendy came out to feed and found Ghost on three legs, a large laceration on the back of his hind leg. The whole leg was grossly swollen and he was almost unable to walk. I came out and quickly realized that the wound was even worse than it looked. It had invaded the tendon sheath and an unchecked infection in this area could be lethal. I cleaned and bandaged the wound, started some aggressive antibiotics and referred him into an equine hospital for surgery.

The surgery went well, but five days later, Ghost developed diarrhea and laminitis, a dangerous disease of the horse's feet. The lamina is the soft tissue attachment between the foot bone and the inside of the hoof wall, and when it becomes inflamed, it is extremely painful for the horse. With enough damage, the lamina can tear and the bone and hoof wall become separated. In extreme cases, the attachments tear all the way around the foot bone causing a life threatening condition known as sinking or "Fatal Sinker Syndrome." Horses in this category have a grim prognosis.

Initially, Ghost didn't seem too bad. Wendy visited him several times and received reassuring reports from the hospital staff. But as time passed, and the vet bills grew larger, Wendy decided to bring him home. The X-rays of his feet taken on the day he came home were horrifying. Ghost was sinking. The bottoms of his hooves bulged with the pressure of the bone pushing from the inside and he was in severe pain.

My friend and certified farrier, Cricket McLaren, CF, had made the long drive to the ranch to help Ghost. Cricket had been Ghost's farrier for years, and was a good friend of the family. He and I had worked closely with George on many laminitis cases, but George was gone now, and neither of us had ever attempted to treat a case this severe.

We looked at each other in dismay, first when we saw the bottoms of his feet, and then when we saw the X-ray images on the computer screen. This was, by far, the worst set of X-rays either of us had seen on a horse that wasn't about to be euthanized. Wendy and her two daughters held onto Ghost as we worked on him and the anguish on their faces was sobering. We had to try to fix this horse. Failure was not an option!

Cricket shod Ghost with heart bar shoes on all four feet. Ghost was taken off all medications, for if he continued to stand, logically he would continue to sink and the blood supply to the foot bone would be destroyed and the bone could come through the bottom of his feet. If that happened, we'd have to put him down.

I'd sent the images of Ghost's feet to some colleagues in Idaho who'd known George well and embraced his methods, and their response was disheartening. They thought we'd most likely lost the blood supply to his feet, as the coffin bones had sunk past a reasonable point, and they did not think we'd be able to save him. I shared their feedback with Cricket, who knew and respected them tremendously, and I could see the discouragement in his face. We agreed that we would not try to be heroes or operate from our own egos. If things were not going the right way, we'd have to euthanize Ghost.

It was a great time to pray. I asked God for guidance and for the wisdom to do what was best for Ghost. I also told God that if he ran into George to feel free to pass along any tips or pointers that Dr. Platt might have. I could picture George dancing up and down somewhere on the other side yelling about Bute.

Thirty-six hours after the medications wore off, Ghost

finally laid down. He stayed down for 35 days! Wendy was steadfast in her nursing care. Ghost was thickly bedded, first on wood shavings, then on straw, which worked better for padding. Wendy hand-fed and watered him multiple times a day, and when the first snow flew, moved him inside to a double stall, bedded with about four feet of straw. The wound on the hind leg still needed bandaging, and she tended to that as well.

Ghost's care took a long time every day, but Wendy never complained, nor questioned us or demanded predictions that no one could make. She was steadfast, knowing that we were taking the only chance we had. She'd known George for years, and had trusted him completely, and transferred that great trust to Cricket and me.

Ghost was a great patient initially. He'd eat his hay lying flat on his side, a calm look in his eye. He was never agitated or distressed, just wanted to sleep most of the time. He'd get up to change sides or to urinate or defecate – otherwise he was lying down. Wendy would hold buckets of gruel and mash for him and he'd stick his nose into the slurry, eat what he wanted, then fling his head, throwing goo everywhere.

He never developed colic, the horseman's term for belly ache, and did just fine lying down for most of the day. Cricket and I would stop in, separately and at random times, each of us watching and waiting for an indication that Ghost could be saved. We'd eat our lunch sitting on the ground next to him. Ghost seemed to welcome the company, lounging on his thick straw mattress like royalty. I could almost picture him waving a foot and saying, "Beulah, peel me a grape!"

At the four-week mark, Ghost's shoes were reset and he was X-rayed again. The soles of his feet were markedly thicker and the tip of the foot bone looked good, letting us know that there was no infection present in the bone. The separation of hoof wall and bone was obvious on the X-rays, and there was also free fluid in his feet, most likely from old blood from the torn laminae. Although the sinking had ceased, his coffin bones showed severe rotation, presumably from the pull of the deep digital flexor tendon. He stood for the procedures, but he swayed and shifted his weight, still in severe pain.

We cut away some hoof wall to drain the fluid and brownish watery liquid bubbled out as Ghost shifted weight from foot to foot. He was markedly improved after relieving the pressure in his feet, but was happy to collapse onto his straw bed after we were finished.

We all agreed that we'd keep trying until Ghost let us know it was time to stop. No one wanted to make him suffer any longer than he already had, but something in his look told us that he was battling to live. As long as he had that light in his eye, we'd fight for him.

Cricket and I spent long hours on the phone discussing Ghost and what to do next. We really were feeling our way forward with this case, and we supported each other constantly. Whatever plan we made was made together. We would bounce new ideas off each other and discuss what was working, what wasn't working and why.

I had to come back 10 days later and remove almost the entire front of his hoof walls on both front feet, as they were necrotic and full of pus. I wasn't sure how stable the remaining foot was, given that there was no attachment between the bone and the hoof walls, and I crossed my fingers the whole way home that the feet wouldn't suddenly collapse. Again, I needed to ask George so many questions, and I couldn't.

Wendy added soaking and wrapping Ghost's feet to her list of duties without complaint. Ghost was not cooperative for either. He'd jerk his feet away and slam them down hard, and pull back violently in the cross ties. Wendy kept excellent nursing records during this time, and they were peppered with expletives.

One set of notes read, "He must have hit his head six times pulling back. Broke the cross ties. Dork! Not eating at 10 p.m. Maybe his head hurts."

Another nursing note read, "Duct tape slippers holding up pretty good. Once again, a real [expletive] about his feet! Unbelievable how stupid he can be! I almost think he enjoys slamming his head into the beams!"

Adding to the ordeal, temperatures were now regularly below freezing and the barn was not heated. Ghost had lost almost 175 pounds and we worried about pneumonia on top of everything else.

When the shoes were pulled for the next reset, Ghost's soles on the front feet came off as well. Underneath the sloughed sole was infected necrotic debris and the smell was awful. Fortunately, after everything was cleaned out, there was healthy tissue present, and a strong pulse in the arteries let us know that at least the blood supply was intact.

Wendy wrote, "Cricket pulled the heart bars off and [Ghost's] sole came off with it. Lovely sight. All the dead laminae sloughing off. So now he has literally no soles and guess what? We get to soak all four feet! Goody! But they were very happy with his progress. I was a little in horror but I trust them ..."

We reset the shoes, one foot at a time, and Ghost looked the best yet, standing calmly in the barn aisle, all four feet pulled squarely under him. The calm look in his eye told me everything I needed to know. He was going to make it through this! He would live! But could he ever be sound again? None of us dared to hope.

This was the turning point, and from here, the recovery sped along, the feet looking better each week as the tissue granulated in and the soles grew back. Ghost began to venture out into the field, each day going farther. At first he stayed away from the herd, but he eased closer and closer, and finally he was among them, picking up his old rank. The whole family was there on the February day that Ghost was trotted in hand for the first time, and I filmed the event. Ghost ran past the camera, smooth and sound!

I advised the family to start bringing Ghost along on a lead rope when they went out for rides on the ranch. They also started trailering him to the indoor arena with the other horses, letting him just be present for the work. He gained weight and his coat began to shine.

Finally it was time to take Ghost for his first ride. It had been almost five months since the ordeal had started, and no one knew how he'd feel under saddle. Wendy took it slow at first, but Ghost was ready to return to the things he used to do, and to everyone's amazement, he loped around the arena without a trace of lameness, doing flying lead changes with ease.

Today, Ghost is back in competition, running barrels, winning money, roping and doing what he does best – being ornery. It was real teamwork that saved Ghost. Cricket, Wendy and I each had a job to do, and if one of us had failed in our duties, Ghost would not have survived. However, Ghost himself deserves a lot of the credit. His will to live was indomitable. Plus, I have a feeling Dr. Platt was somewhere, whispering in all of our ears when times were tough. If it weren't for George's methods, we would have lost Ghost.

The three of us wrote the case up and it was published in the July/August 2013 American Farrier's Journal. Ghost has his own Facebook page, "Ghost the Horse," and updates on his progress are posted regularly. There are also photos and video clips from the ordeal.

Ghost was taken out of heart bar shoes in August 2013 and placed in regular shoes, and he performed well all summer and fall. His shoes will be removed for the 2013-14 winter, leaving him barefoot for the first time since the ordeal. He's ready.

It isn't often that an owner comes along who is willing and

able to nurse a downed horse for so long, and performs all treatments diligently and without complaint, and who trusts me enough to stay on board for such a long, arduous process. Wendy Parker deserves a standing ovation for being a great client. Cricket deserves the same for being a great farrier. And George Platt, DVM deserves all the credit for showing us how to treat laminitis, and never faltering in his convictions. George was unstoppable, and he changed me, Wendy, Cricket and Ghost forever.

# Afterword

While all of the stories and events in this book were taken from real life, some details and locations were changed to protect the privacy of the individuals. I have also taken the liberty of combining similar stories into one whenever possible.

There's a lot to laugh about when you're a veterinarian and there are a lot of wonderful clients who make it all worth it. To each and every wonderful client in my life, you know who you are, and from the bottom of my heart, thank you! I am so grateful for your presence in my life!

The characters in the "Clients from Hell" portion are a compilation of traits from a number of similar personality types that I have encountered over the years and were not modeled after any one specific person. If you think you recognize yourself in any of these characters, perhaps it's time to detoxify and work on being a better human being. If you were offended by these stories, you probably need to be offended more often.

To my colleagues and fellow equine professionals who are feeling the pain of having to deal with some of these personality types, don't take them personally. Easier said than done, especially when they launch personal attacks on us, but it is possible. Just remember that every human being that we encounter is living inside his or her own reality, not ours. Try praying for someone who has hurt you – it will turn the situation around in ways you've never imagined possible.

Let's all do our best and keep our side of the street clean. Let's avoid cynicism. Let's be kind to one another and be accountable for our actions. And bringing God along as we go through life can only make things better. May you find him now!

If you are a veterinarian struggling with addiction or with suicidal thoughts, you are not alone, and you might be surprised by how many other veterinarians also struggle, particularly those who seem to have it all together. Isolation is the most deadly factor in a person's path to suicide. If you are feeling alone and need a friend to talk to, send me a message on my Facebook page: https://www.facebook.com/CourtneySDiehlDvmMobileVeterinaryServices. I would love to hear from you! If you are thinking of harming yourself or taking your life, PLEASE call the National Suicide Prevention Hotline at 800-273-8255

One day, I would like to work in a barn full of all sorts of horses and all types of riders, and witness everyone getting along and offering support and kindness to each other. But it's got to start with the barn management, and if they are corrupt, there's no hope for the barn. Corrupt barn management seems to be the norm, unfortunately.

If a boarding barn can breed witches and evildoing, it can also breed respect, harmony and peace. Come to think of it, that would be a great horse story.

Maybe I will get to tell it someday.

# **Acknowledgements**

Dr. Diehl and Eve

I am indebted to the following people for inspiring and encouraging me to complete this book:

To my husband Jim, and my daughters Sunny and Morgan, who endured my long nights at the computer and long days at work or on emergencies.  Your support and love means the world, and any day now I'll confess that book number two is in the works.

To my mother, who has read everything I've sent her and been honest and constructive with her feedback. Thank you for all of the years of support and encouragement, love and patience, and for sharing your wisdom with me!

To Barbara Logan, for excellent feedback and ideas, and for always being there for us.

To Cornelia Platt and Sadie, Betsy and Ross Rectenwald, Connie, Kelley and Andy Platt, Erin and Henry Rectenwald, and all of George's beloved grandchildren of whom he was so proud. Having all of you out there keeps George alive, and thank you all for sharing him with the rest of the world.

To Jillian, Candace and Amy, for riding in the vet truck, and not quitting when I'm driving with the phone in my ear, and trying to write and eat at the same time. Thanks for helping me make my mobile practice successful and for supporting and believing in me.

To Dr. John and Carolyn Rule, for being great examples for the vets in this small town.

To Tom Riney, CJF, Cricket McLaren, CF and Justin Frank, CJF, three great farriers I have been privileged to work alongside. Thank you for being excellent in every way and sharing your knowledge and skills with me.

To Keith and Stace Kramer, for editing my manuscript and for giving me my first professional feedback on my book. That was a major milestone for me and I will never forget it.

To Dawn Obrecht and Eric Landvic, for spiritual advice, wisdom, and for always having the right thing to say at the right time. Thank you, Dawn, for being my first real reader and giving me the first shove towards turning my rough draft into a book.

To the Steamboat Writers Group for listening and giving helpful feedback.

To Sue Leonard, for wisdom shared, and for guiding me to the Bookcrafters, Joe and Jan McDaniel, who transformed a Word doc into a real book.

Dr. Diehl and the tools of her trade 2013

Courtney S. Diehl, DVM has been an equine veterinarian since 2000. She completed a 12 month internship at a private referral practice in Saratoga Springs, NY working primarily with Thoroughbreds. She then owned and operated a solo equine mobile practice in Eagle, CO until 2007, where she partnered with George Platt, DVM. Dr. Platt and Burney Chapman, CJF, were well known for groundbreaking treatment of laminitis using the heart bar shoe. Dr. Diehl went on to complete a Fellowship in Internal Medicine and Critical Care at Hagyard, Davidson, McGee in Lexington, Kentucky in 2007, before returning to Colorado. Dr. Diehl worked closely with Dr. Platt from 2001 until his death in 2011. Diehl and Platt were co-speakers at the American Farrier's Association's annual conference in Portland, Oregon in 2009. In 2012, Diehl and Cricket McLaren, CF successfully treated 'the worst laminitis case of their careers,' not only saving the horse, but returning him to full performance. The case report was published in the July/August 2013 American Farrier's

Journal. Dr. Diehl has been a speaker at several private clinics on laminitis, and spoke at a No Laminitis! conference in Oregon in 2013. She serves on the board of directors of the Colorado Horse Council. Dr. Diehl enjoys spending time with her husband and two daughters, riding her horses and skiing the Steamboat powder when she's not out on calls.

Dr. Diehl and one of her daughters with their horses, 2013

CPSIA information can be obtained at www.ICGtesting.com
Printed in the USA
LVOW12s0526270314

378798LV00003B/6/P